MW00366062

thoughthe**vision**tarry

waiting for my promised mate

aleathea**dupree**

DATHEA
WASHINGTON, D.C.

Book and cover design by Dathea

ISBN 0-9712240-0-5

Published by Dathea
Washington, DC 20012
www.dathea.com
To order additional copies or to contact the author, please email: vision@dathea.com
Printed in the United States of America.

This book is dedicated to:

Those who are waiting for the fulfillment of a promise
that God has given to you.
God will do just what He says.

My friends and loved ones who are still waiting
for their promised mates.
If He did it for me, He'll do it for you too!

Wayne and Priscilla
My favorite couple. Keep up the good work.

Faith
My faithful witness down through the years.
Thank you for your friendship.

Marie
For always encouraging and supporting me.
You're the best sister.

My husband, David
You were worth the wait.

Foreword by Bishop Alfred A. Owens, Jr., D.Min., Senior Pastor
Greater Mount Calvary Holy Church, Washington, D.C.

God created people to long for relationship with others. By our very nature, we are relational creatures longing to be in fellowship with each other. However, most important among these coveted relationships is the marital covenant. Accentuating this desire is society's notion that men and women are not complete until they are married. Our innate longing coupled with society's urging usually results in an overwhelming number of people who are prematurely rushing to the altar.

Needless to say, this very same rushed recipe of relationship is at the root of the alarming divorce rate that not only plagues secular society, but even the Lord's Church! In fact, many marriages end in divorce rather than in the proverbial "happily ever after" scenario made famous by fairytales.

I am excited to declare that "happily ever after" is not just a fairytale, but God's desire for all married couples. However, there are prerequisites for this coveted marital bliss. Most important among these prerequisites is waiting not only for God's intended mate, but also waiting until we are mature enough, being both mentally and spiritually prepared. I believe that this lesson in patience is the missing ingredient in all too many marriages.

God in His providence, has now brought to the fore an awesome tool that I believe will help many who are contemplating marriage. Aleathea Dupree, with a voice of experience and maturity, has penned a great premarital tool. "THOUGH THE VISION TARRY: Waiting For My Promised Mate" is a God-inspired book that is a must-read for anyone considering the prospect of marriage as well as those already married.

The subject that this book broaches is very relevant. The message of patience that God has placed in Aleathea Dupree is a timely message to this generation. In this powerful work that illustrates God's mighty power to bring His promise to pass, the author sheds light on the promise available to every Christian. I am convinced that the principles illuminated in this book will be a blessing in the life of the reader.

an introductory word about waiting

'Wait' is a very peculiar word. It can imply a thrilling suspense or a dreadful prolonging. How we interpret the word has to do with *who* or *what* we are waiting for and *how* we wait for it. If we are waiting for something or someone pleasant, waiting can be interpreted as a joyful expectancy. However, if we are waiting for the unpleasant, waiting can bring anxiety, fear and distress.

We have often heard that when we pray, God will provide us with one of three answers: 'Yes', 'No', or 'Wait', the latter being the answer we very seldom want to hear. Judging by some people's reactions, to wait on the Lord is often thought of as a negative response when in fact it is God's way of encouraging and teaching us. Our waiting can be a time of rest and enjoyment if we keep in mind *Who* we are waiting for. Many of us make ourselves weary with worry, wondering what and how long the waiting is for. But we have to remember that it is the Lord we are waiting for and when He tells us to wait, there is always something great in store. God never tells us to wait to punish us, but to give us rest. Even so, many of us refuse to accept His rest. Instead, we pace to and fro, and waste what could be useful and productive time.

Have you ever been to a train station? Most of the people there are waiting for the train to come, though not all are expecting to go to the same place. Some people prefer to have a seat while they're waiting, some read a book, and some even catch a quick nap. But others, even though a seat may be available, prefer to stand or walk back and forth from the wall to the edge of the track to peer down the tunnel to see whether or not the train is coming. By the time the train arrives, these people are tired, irritable, and very frustrated... but they still had to wait. Understandably, some people are anxious to reach their destination, but realistically, no matter what we do, we do not have the power to make that train reach us any faster. Some might argue that we can, in effect, make the train reach us faster by running towards it, but I'm sure after a little thought we would all agree that running towards a moving train is not the smartest thing to do!

How do *you* wait for the Lord? Do you pace anxiously to and fro? Do you run foolishly toward what you should have been waiting for? Do you rest in your waiting? Waiting can be one of the most pleasant and restful experiences. It all depends on *how* you wait. One thing is certain, when God tells us to wait, we can be assured of three things: 1) He *will* come; 2) He will come *on time* (His time); and 3) He will never tell us to wait for something not *worth waiting for*. If we keep these things in mind, we can rejoice and be thankful in our waiting!

This book is for those of you who are waiting for the fulfillment of a promise that God has given to you. It is my prayer that through the testimony that God has given me, you will be encouraged, strengthened and challenged. Hopefully you will learn from my experiences and avoid the pitfalls and traps that ensnared me. Most importantly, my prayer is that you will learn the lessons that God is teaching you during your time of waiting. If you are already experiencing a season of fulfillment, use this book as a reference for future promises that the Lord will give to you.

The next time you are encouraged by the Lord to wait, accept

His encouragement and challenges to grow with gratitude and joyful anticipation. But please, whatever you do, stay away from the track, and don't run toward any moving trains!

acknowledgments

I would like to thank all of those who contributed their time, editing skills, and much needed feedback and encouragement to the completion of this project: Mary Dumas, Claretta Dupree, Marie Jones, and Faith Messado.

I would also like to thank Andrea Jayne Poyser for prompting me to tell her my story. The "epistle-like" answers to your questions laid the framework for this book.

To my pastors, Bishop Alfred A. Owens, Jr. and Evangelist Susie C. Owens, and the Washington, D.C. Greater Mount Calvary Holy Church family: thank you for your encouragement and support.

And to my beloved husband, David, who put up with me and this book when we were both "in the raw." I couldn't have done this without you. Because you are in my life, yet another portion of the vision has been realized. Thanks for your love and patience, and thanks for dreaming big dreams for me.

CONTENTS

1

redflags

Hindsight does not always have twenty-twenty vision, but it can. How? By taking an honest look at our past experiences. We must look at what went wrong, how we contributed to what went wrong, what we have learned from our experience, and what steps we need to take in order to prevent making the same mistakes in the future. There are warning signs along the highways and byways of life, yet sometimes our lack of knowledge and experience causes us to miss them. Hindsight becomes insight when we allow ourselves to heal and grow from past mistakes, and insight becomes foresight when we apply the lessons learned from our past to our future.

This book is about the realization of a vision that God gave me. The realization of my vision required hindsight, foresight, and insight because it was birthed out of a nightmare, but ended up being a wonderful dream come true. My hindsight has twenty-twenty vision, but it wasn't always that way. Here's how it all started.

In December of 1990 I attended the wedding of a dear friend of mine. As she and her husband-to-be were about to take their vows, I was struck by the admonition of their pastor when he said, "Marriage is not to be entered into unadvisedly." The statement struck a chord within me! The word 'unadvisedly' means 'having received no advice; not informed; carried out without *careful* deliberation.' This suggests that before you marry you should receive some (good) advice; you should have some information about yourself, your potential partner, and marriage itself. Marriage should not be entered into without careful deliberation. When you get a chance, look up the words 'careful' and 'deliberation' in a dictionary. If you're in a relationship and considering marriage, think of this as a required homework assignment.

It dawned on me for the first time that the decision to marry and marriage itself is such an important undertaking that it requires careful, deliberate consideration and wise counsel. I had never thought about marriage in those terms until that moment. I began to think back on my own life and the decisions I had made concerning marriage. I had not received advice, I did not have enough information, and I certainly entered into it without careful deliberation. I was one who, because of ignorance, was unable to see the warning signs. But that day at the wedding of my friend, my vision began to clear.

At that time I had been separated for two years, a year longer than I had been married. Why did I end up separated after only a year of marriage? Hindsight has taught me that red flags were waving before I got married. How did I end up in the situation I was in? In a nutshell, I had "entered in unadvisedly." Here are a few specifics about some of the areas that proved to be the most detrimental.

When I got married I had just turned twenty-two and I had lived a fairly sheltered life. I was brought up in the church and knew of God, but I did not know God. After a brief period of resistance, I accepted the Lord at the age of fifteen. Even though (and probably because) I became a Christian at a young age, after seven years of being in the church there was a lot I had not been exposed to. At age twenty-two, I was not an immature person overall, but I still had a lot to learn about relationships. I was in my last year of college and certainly still at a very formative stage of my emotional, physical, mental, spiritual, and social development. I did not have a clear concept of who I was yet, much less who I wanted to spend the rest of my life with. Some people are very mature at that age and are prepared for the life-long commitment of marriage to another person. I was not one of them. First red flag.

I thought I had a pretty good relationship with the Lord, but there were a lot of things that I did not know, and some of the things that I did know were not fully understood. I certainly did not understand God's design for marriage. It's so tragic that many of us spend little or no time preparing for marriage, but we'll spend time and energy preparing for things that are a lot less significant in comparison. Take driving a car for example. We all know (those of us who are lawful) that before we can get our driver's license, we need to study and learn what driving is all about, what rules are involved, and what the best driving practices are. The hope is that after passing the test we will be examples of informed and safe drivers, and consequently avoid causing harm to ourselves or someone else. Entering into marriage, on the other hand, is a lot of times not even given the same consideration as learning to drive a car! As a result, many marriages end up wrecked; sometimes with casualties.

Some little girls dream about the kind of man that they hope to marry, but I never did that. I had my share of adolescent boyfriend-girlfriend relationships, but in reality, I had only two "adult" relationships prior to this—one at the age of eighteen and the other at the age of twenty—and the only thing I took away from both of them was an experience of distrust. I did not understand the dynamics involved in a good male-female relationship. I did not know anything about developing a friendship, or trust, or getting to know about what makes the other person who they are (their background, beliefs, family, personality, experiences, etc.). I knew nothing about the importance of communication, or the progressing stages of a relationship, or goals, plans, and ambitions. Nothing! To complicate matters, the church I grew up in taught that once you met and began to go out with someone (i.e. to court or date them with the intention of marriage), you were to get married within six months. I suppose that in some strange way the time limit was to ensure a good and godly relationship. Even though I had an extra six months in my relationship, the time constraint was not a helpful factor. Not only did I lack a clear picture of who I was, what kind of person would be best suited for me, and who I would be best suited for, I did not allow enough time to develop a friendship and really get to know the person I ended up marrying. More red flags.

The man I married (who I'll refer to as 'Mr. Ex') professed to be a born again believer, but here's another red flag: Mr. Ex had only been saved for a year and prior to that was completely unchurched. I say he "professed" to have been a born again believer because he *appeared* to have had a genuine conversion experience. What I did not understand then was that when a tree starts to bud, it takes time to see what kind of fruit will be produced, and when someone becomes a born again believer, it takes time to see the fruit of genuine conversion.

After becoming a "Christian," Mr. Ex became quite active in the church: he ushered, sang in the choir, attended fasting and prayer services every Monday, prayer meeting and Bible study every Wednesday, and worship services every Sunday. But, believe it or not, that was not enough. Just because a person participates in "church related" activities does not mean he or she is in a right relationship with God. Christ said there will be many on the day of judgment who will try to use church related activity as a means of justifying themselves. This is what Christ said in Matthew 7:21-23:

> "Not everyone who says to me, 'Lord, Lord,' will enter the kingdom of heaven, but only he who does the will of my Father who is in heaven. Many will say to me on that day, 'Lord, Lord, did we not prophesy in your name, and in your name drive out demons and perform many miracles?' Then I will tell them plainly, 'I never knew you...'"

There's an expression that says, "Time has a big mouth and if you give something enough time, it will tell you everything you need to know." How true this is. I had not known Mr. Ex long before he started coming to church. As a matter of fact, he came to church because of me (another possible red flag). That in itself was not a negative thing, but it does take time to uncover a person's true motive.

Everyone was impressed with Mr. Ex's zeal and faithful attendance, but all that glittered was not gold. I may not have been unequally yoked with an unbeliever (as far as I could ascertain at that time), but I did not realize at that time the importance of yoking up with someone who could be my spiritual head. Mr. Ex was not in a position to be my spiritual head: another red flag. The fact that I yoked up with someone who for the most part I ended up instructing and nurturing distorted the blueprint for marriage that God has ordained.

Yet another red flag was the relationship that Mr. Ex had with his family. It was not a good one. He did not live with or really know his father. Sadly, that's not altogether unusual in our times and culture. The lack of a father does not necessarily make you a poor candidate for marriage, but the lack of authority and accountability does. He also had a poor relationship with his mother. It was actually through our relationship, and through the intervention of my own mother that he realized the importance of, and improved his relationship with his own mother. It is said that if you want some insight into how a man may treat you as his wife, take a look at how he treats his own mother.

Mr. Ex also had very low self-esteem. (I've lost count as to which number red flag this is). Do not, I repeat, *do not* marry if low self-esteem is an issue for you or for the person with whom you are or might become involved. When I refer to a person with 'low self-esteem' I'm referring to the person who is unwilling to realize his or her own value. A person who cannot see any worth in himself or herself cannot fully value another person's worth. This is a very important issue that should be addressed before marriage is even considered.

Because of Mr. Ex's low self-esteem, I spent most of my time propping him up, instructing him, and trying to bolster his ego. You do enough ego bolstering with a man who has a healthy self-concept, so you can imagine what it's like to be with a man who already has major issues with himself—it's draining to say the least!

6

Mr. Ex's lack of self-esteem fostered within him a sense of insecurity, which fostered an environment of secrecy, which fostered an attitude of selfishness, jealousy, and anger. Red flags five through ten! It was a downward spiral and I got caught in it. Some of these traits I saw only a glimpse of before marriage. But where there's smoke, there's fire, and I was about to learn that the fire in him was burning out of control in more ways than one.

When Mr. Ex approached my mother and stated his intention to marry me (note: he did not state his *desire* to marry me, but his *intention*—there is a difference) my mother laughed out loud. She just couldn't take him seriously because we had only been seeing each other for a few months at that point. When my mother told me of Mr. Ex's intentions I laughed out loud as well, and for the same reason. But he was determined and persistent, which, by the way, are sometimes the traits of "Mr. Wrong." Anyone that is in too much of a hurry to get married should give you cause for alarm. His impatience was yet another red flag.

As time went on, the relationship got serious and we eventually did get engaged. We were both young and dumb, and neither one of us knew what to expect. It was our church's practice to present newly engaged couples to the congregation. When our engagement was announced, we assumed that we would automatically be called in for premarital counseling. We waited for a while to be called in but when the call never came, we decided to be proactive and ask for counseling. That was the one thing we *did* do right. Unfortunately, we did not get what we expected. When we went in for what we thought would be our first counseling session, it went *exactly* like this:

Counselor: (to him) "Is everyone in agreement?"

Mr. Ex: "Yes."

Counselor: (to me) "Is everyone in agreement?"

Me: "Yes."

Counselor: (to us) "Okay, let's pray."

That was it! We did not even sit down! After the prayer, we were dismissed with best wishes. Needless to say, after this whole experience (the half of which has not yet been told, but keep reading) I am now a staunch advocate of pre-marital counseling. At that time, I was so sheltered, I did not even know that there were other churches where we could have gone in order to get the counseling we needed. Proper counseling is key! It's like studying the driver's manual before taking the test. Pre-marital counseling should teach you what marriage is all about, what rules are involved, and what the best practices are. Without wise counsel, you increase your chances of your marriage ending up wrecked with you as a casualty.

Well, somehow or another we made it through the wedding planning, and the big day came. The wedding was beautiful, but little did I know the hell I was about to enter into... and it didn't take long.

thenightmare

Mr. Ex's true colors began to show immediately after we were married. The once zealous and faithful church attendee began to find excuses for not going to church. Not all at once, but little by little his participation in church activities began to dwindle. Instead of going to Bible study, fasting and prayer, and Sunday morning worship, he preferred to stay at home and watch football and other things. The ushering eventually stopped, participation in the choir eventually stopped, and church was no longer a priority. It was bad enough (and frightening enough) that Mr. Ex was no longer a faithful churchgoer, but what made it worse was that he made it as difficult as possible for me to attend.

My relationship with the Lord has always kept me going; second to that is my love of music. The very things that Mr. Ex knew were important to me seemed to be the things that were targeted for destruction. I could no longer freely go to choir rehearsals without coming home to all sorts of accusations and ranting. My desire to go to church became a measure of my loyalty to him. Mr. Ex was jealous of my relationship with God and of any activity I was involved in that had anything to do with God.

He became abusive: physically, verbally, and mentally. It started small with things like his blocking my path to prevent me from moving in a direction that he did not want me to move in, to grabbing my arm in the heat of an argument, to outright physical violence, some aspects of which were brutal. After a few months of increasing violence, I still refused to give up on my marriage. I did the best thing that I knew how to do: I prayed. I prayed that my marriage would be what I thought it should be (even though I was still uninformed at that point). I prayed for a change in Mr. Ex's behavior, and I prayed that he would be the man that God wanted him to be. In spite of all my praying, the situation continued to worsen.

I never dreamed that I would find myself in a position where I was being abused. I was one who said that I would never allow a man to put his hands on me. But it's a whole different situation once you're in an abusive situation and living it. Most of the time the violence caught me completely off-guard and many times my best response was to be completely shocked. The worst abuse seemed to be strategic in its attack and would usually occur when I was in the best of moods, or just coming home from church or school (yes, I was still in my last year of college at the time). It would sometimes seem as if he would stay at home and think of the most wicked and vile things, convince himself that they were true, and then vent his rage on me as soon as I walked in the door.

The pattern was always the same. He would work up a rage, become abusive, blame me for his own abusive behavior, then follow with a period of tearful penitence, declaring his love and promising never to do it again. The promises were always broken, and each subsequent incident became more violent than the last.

I did not tell anyone about the abuse, and my silence proved to be one of his greatest allies. For starters, I didn't know who to tell. I thought that if I told my family they would never forgive him, even if his behavior later changed for the better. Secondly, I felt that talking to someone else about his bad behavior would be like a betrayal. The only person I felt safe in talking to was God.

After a few months of marriage, I made another tragic discovery. It happened one Sunday afternoon when we planned to have some of his family over for dinner. I had come home from church (alone), and we decided to rent some videos to watch for that afternoon. He offered to ride to the video store with me but said he would stay in the car. On the way there, he made a point of requesting that I rent some Christian videos, which was fine with me. After picking out the videos I wanted, I went up to the front desk to check them out. The man behind the counter asked me if I had returned the movies that had been previously rented. Since that was the first time I was using that particular video card, I didn't know what he was talking about, but I followed my instincts. I asked him if videos had been rented on the card before, and he let me know that videos were rented "all the time." When I asked the man what kind of videos had been rented, his face turned beet red as he told me that the titles of the videos were so obscene he could not tell me what they were. He could only tell me that they were extremely pornographic.

At that moment, it seemed as if the blood ran cold in my veins and I felt a chill go through my body. I thanked him for the information, finished checking out the videos I was renting, and left the store. When I went back to the car, Mr. Ex was searching my face for any revelatory expressions, but he found none. We drove back to the house, and went through the afternoon as planned. Though I had not said anything, Mr. Ex began to suspect that something was wrong, and he began to follow me around the house trying to get me to say out loud what he feared I had discovered. It was this discovery that became my breaking point—I couldn't handle it. It seems strange to say that even though I was suffering under the physical abuse, knowing that he was involved in pornography was the worst discovery yet. In my mind, it was marital unfaithfulness. As far as I was concerned, I could not live with that and I told Mr. Ex as much.

After our guests had gone home, I spoke freely of how I felt. I had no desire to live with Mr. Ex any longer. He pleaded with me to stay with him and I continued to refuse, but after hours of pleading and promises to never have anything to do with the pornography (and other bad behavior), I agreed to give him another chance. After that he was on his best behavior for a while, but as with most abusers who take no concrete steps to really change, the abuse eventually resurfaced. One Sunday, a few weeks later, after leaving Mr. Ex at home, on an impulse I decided to drive back to the house. On my way back home I saw Mr. Ex heading for the video store. I later confronted him and confirmed that he was still renting pornographic videos.

The abuse took many forms. Because of Mr. Ex's jealous insecurity, he trusted me with no one and wanted me all to himself. He was completely obsessed. He once told me that he wished that he could keep me locked up in a room that only he could access. This, according to him, was an expression of love. He did not want me to spend time with anyone: my friends, family (mine or his)—

no one! I knew I was in trouble when he told me that he loved me more than God. That was the most frightening statement anyone could have said to me. In his mind I was his world, and he convinced himself that he could not go on unless I was a part of his life. Now faced with the threat of my leaving him (because of his continued abusive behavior), he began to threaten my life. After a while I heard the phrase: "If you ever leave me, I'll kill you and kill myself" at least two or three times a week, and I believed that he did mean it.

Months passed and the situation continued to worsen. The physical abuse was getting increasingly more violent, and I eventually reached the point where I felt that I could take no more. I no longer felt any love towards Mr. Ex and even he could see that things were just not working. We sat down together one day, and he gave me a nice speech about how he knew that he was not treating me right and he offered to leave and get a place of his own with hopes of working things out. I told him he needed to get some help, but I could not promise that we would get back together because I did not know if he would take the necessary steps to change. At any rate, our discussion ended amicably. I actually felt more hopeful then than I had in a long time, and he seemed encouraged by the possibility of a better future. But... that bright and happy moment didn't last long.

During the period when he was looking for a place of his own, I came home from school one day to find Mr. Ex brooding in a dark room. As I headed up the stairs he began to accuse me. He seemed to have successfully convinced himself that I had found someone else. In an attempt to assure him that his accusation was not true, I gave him as cheerful a response as I could muster, and headed for another room. But Mr. Ex was not to be appeased. He was working himself up into a fury, and I knew that he had to convince himself of such things in order to feed his rage. What followed was the worst of our most violent episodes. I was beat up, dragged down the stairs, locked in a room, held at knife point, stripped, choked, and almost raped. I prayed that day like I had *never* prayed before! I thought it was the end for me, but God preserved my life. When it was over, it was over. I finally broke my silence, and by the end of the next day, police were escorting Mr. Ex out of the house under the authority of a restraining order.

I was devastated! This was not how I thought my marriage would end. I believed in "until death do us part," but I didn't expect that it would be my own husband that would be trying to effectuate the death clause! I entered into marriage with the best of intentions. I had prayed and asked for God's blessings; I had married someone that I believed was saved; I had done what I thought was right to do. Why did this happen? The answer is simple to state, but difficult to live: God allowed it.

Do you remember the story of Joseph? Joseph was not a perfect person, but he was committed to God and God had a plan for his life. God gave Joseph a wonderful dream that pertained to his future. God gave Him this dream knowing that this young man, (who in my opinion lacked discretion), would relate his dream to his brothers. God knew that the telling of this dream would fuel jealousy in Joseph's brothers to the point that they would conspire to kill him. He was thrown into a pit, sold into slavery, falsely accused, then thrown into prison, and forgotten about. I'm sure there were times when Joseph wondered why these things were happening to him, but Joseph eventually gained twenty-twenty hindsight. Joseph learned that God had a plan. God had allowed all these things to happen to Joseph in order to bring him to the place where the purpose that God had for him could be fulfilled. When Joseph learned this, he was able to tell his brothers that even though they meant him harm, God allowed it for good.

When my hindsight became twenty-twenty, I was able to say the same thing: what Mr. Ex, and ultimately Satan, meant for my destruction, God meant it for my good! God was with me *in* the fire. I remember times when I was hit and slammed repeatedly against walls and God protected me, allowing me to feel impact, but not pain. I could give you testimony after testimony of His miraculous interventions that literally spared me serious bodily harm, and in some instances, saved my life. Before I close this chapter, I want to share a testimony of one of these miraculous interventions.

As believers we often say that we believe that God is the same as He was in olden times, and that He has the same miraculous and delivering power now that He had then. I am living proof that God still miraculously delivers. I am one who knows what it's like to be in the fire and not get burned, and to be in the lions' den and not get devoured. Even though God allowed me to endure a most painful experience, through it all He preserved something that was very precious to me: my *virginity*.

It so happened that my menstrual cycle, which was not due for several weeks, started unexpectedly on the morning of our wedding. When I thought about it later, I chalked it off to stress even though I did not feel particularly stressed at the time. At any rate, Mr. Ex

15

and I did not consummate our marriage when we went away for our honeymoon.

Right after we arrived home from the honeymoon, the Lord spoke to me and in no uncertain terms said that He would not allow the marriage to be consummated. He said, and I quote, "I will not allow it." I don't know how you would have reacted in such a situation, but as for me, I was shocked, stunned, and speechless! I had been looking forward with *great* anticipation to the consummation of my marriage. I had remained a virgin for twenty-two years and I was ready to go forth and enjoy the undefiled marriage bed. But, God said no.

I remember sitting on the edge of what was supposed to have been my "marriage" bed trying to wrap my mind around what God had said. I never questioned Him or thought about rebelling against what He had said, but I couldn't understand it! I tried to make some sense out of it by trying to figure out a reason why God said no. By this time, the abuse had already begun so I thought maybe God was not going to allow the consummation until the abuse stopped. Or, I thought, perhaps I would get pregnant right away and God did not want me to bring a child into an abusive situation. I even wondered if Mr. Ex might have had some dreaded disease that God was protecting me from. I just didn't know!

I never said anything to Mr. Ex about what God had told me. Somehow, I didn't feel the need to tell him. I figured if God wasn't going to allow us to consummate, He would know how to stop it. So I held my peace. My natural physical desires never went away, and I never forbade him in any way... *it just never happened!*

There is a story in the scriptures that reminds me of what

happened to me. The story is found in Genesis chapter 20. In this story Abraham takes his wife Sarah and settles in a different country. While he is there, Abimilech, the king of the country, takes Sarah and intends to make her his wife and consummate the marriage. But God speaks to Abimilech in a dream and tells him that if he tries to consummate with Sarah he's a dead man. Of course, Abimilech does not touch Sarah. The part that I relate to the most is at the end of verse 6 where God says, "I did not let you touch her." (NASB). God would not allow it.

I can't explain what happened to me, and I don't know if God spoke to Mr. Ex the way He spoke to Abimilech. All I know is that God did not allow Mr. Ex to "touch" me and consummate the marriage. He preserved my virginity. I was puzzled about the situation at the time, but later on when I looked back with twenty-twenty hindsight, I was filled with overwhelming gratitude.

God kept me. During the last violent episode when Mr. Ex tried to rape me, when he seemed set on fire by hell itself, even then he could not carry out the act. He was physically able, and he certainly seemed determined enough, but his violent intentions came to an abrupt halt. It was almost as if I could hear God saying, "I told you I will not allow it to happen." Mr. Ex may have had plans of his own, but God had His own plan. And in the end, it's always God's plan that prevails (Proverbs 19:21).

Deliverance does not mean an easy way out. Sometimes deliverance is very painful. My own deliverance was hard, painful, and bloody, but it was still deliverance. God will use the fire of various trials to refine us, to forge character within us, and most importantly, to teach us about Himself. Many times, in order to

17

accomplish God's purpose for our lives we will go through "fiery trials," and we may sometimes find ourselves staring into the lion's mouth, but God knows how to deliver those who are His.

3

trust101

The first two years of my separation were full of torment for me. I was still terrified because I still believed that Mr. Ex was planning to take my life (and I found out later that he actually was). He had made so many threats on my life when we were together that I knew he would try to kill or disfigure me if he had the chance. It was during this time that the Lord started what I call my "higher education" courses, the first of which was Trust 101.

The night the police came to remove Mr. Ex I was so terrified of him that, even though the police and some of my family members were there, I stayed upstairs until he was taken from the house. I was a nervous wreck!

I remember that same night I was so nervous that when a branch brushed against the bedroom window, I jumped right out of bed and ran towards the door. My nerves were shattered, and I was convinced that Mr. Ex would make good on all of his threats. I was completely devastated.

In addition to being a complete wreck, I felt like I was dying of grief, not so much over Mr. Ex per se, but over what had become of my marriage. I felt a pain inside that I couldn't describe, nor could I tell you exactly where it was. I was in a state of emotional torment and I could not stop crying.

I lay there that night for a while until I couldn't stand it any longer, then I got up, knelt beside the bed, and began to pray. I told God that I didn't see how I could continue to serve Him while being in so much pain inside, and I asked Him to please take the pain away. That's about all I could manage to say before I crawled back into bed and cried myself to sleep.

The next morning when I woke up I felt a change on the inside—I could not feel the pain I felt just the night before. The absence of the pain was so real that I actually clutched my chest, as if to make sure it was really gone, and sure enough, it was! That was just another of the many miracles that God worked on my behalf. I never experienced that pain ever again. The memories were there, as they are now, but the pain had been completely and totally erased. From that day until now, I have never had to shed another tear because of the pain I felt over all that had happened. The pain was gone... but the fear was still there.

Trust 101 started with me learning to lean on scripture instead of physical weapons. Mr. Ex was stalking me in spite of the restraining order. I remember one particular instance when I was at home preparing to leave for work. The phone rang and I had a horrible feeling it was Mr. Ex so I would not answer the phone. Not long after, I heard a knock at the door. I froze in fear because my instincts told me that it was him. The knocking stopped after a minute or so and I immediately called my neighbor to ask her if she could see who was at my front door. I asked her specifically if it was Mr. Ex and she said that she thought it was him, but he was not at the door anymore.

I was really frightened at that point and I didn't know what to do. If it was Mr. Ex he would know I was at home because my car was parked in the driveway. I had to go to work but I was afraid to leave the house in case he was still somewhere nearby. I didn't want to call the police unless I was sure it was him. At that moment the Lord spoke to me and told me to put the top lock on the front door and to check the back door. You can believe what you want, but God does speak, and that's exactly what He told me. I immediately ran downstairs and quickly locked the top lock. When I checked the back door it was not only unlocked, but open as well. I closed it, locked it, and went back upstairs.

Not even a minute later there was a knocking at the door again. This time the knocking didn't stop but instead grew louder and more persistent. Then to my horror I heard a key turn in the bottom lock. The lock was successfully opened, but what prevented the intruder from coming in was the top lock that I had just locked only a few minutes before. You see, the top lock on our house didn't work properly: you could lock and unlock it from the inside, but none of the keys would open it from the outside. Had I not followed God's instruction to lock the top lock I do not believe that I would be alive today. But that's not the end of the story.

When the intruder realized that he could not get in, he left. After waiting a while, I decided to venture out of the house so that I could get to work. I peeped outside and as far as I could see the way looked clear. I checked under and around my car, got in, and started the drive for work. But, I didn't get very far.

I lived in a cul-de-sac, which meant that the same road that was used to enter the cul-de-sac was also used to exit onto the main road. I stopped the car at the stop sign that was at the exit of the cul-de-sac, and just as I made the turn onto the main road, there a few feet ahead of me on the sidewalk, was Mr. Ex. When I saw him, I felt a combination of shock and paralyzing fear. Without thinking, I stepped on the brake pedal. When he saw the car slow down, he quickly approached the car and tried to open the door so that he could "talk to me." By then, my fight or flight mechanisms kicked in, flight being the most predominant, and I drove off. I was not about to let him get into that car!

I had gone only about a mile or so when the Lord spoke to me again and told me to go back to the house. I was still scared and I wondered if Mr. Ex was still there (remember, the top lock was not locked anymore). I decided to drive around the back of the house to see if he might be lurking out of sight, but there was no sign of him. I drove around to the front of the house and I saw no one. I parked in front of my neighbor's house, got out, and just as I was telling her to call the police if she saw him, Mr. Ex came strolling down the street towards my house. How he missed my car I do not know because it was parked directly in front of his line of vision. My neighbor and I watched in disbelief as he boldly walked up to the house, used the key (which, by the way, he was not supposed to have in his possession anymore) and went in.

We called the police and after explaining that a restraining order was being violated, within minutes several police cars pulled up in front of the house. I came out and told them what had happened and they said they would go in and search the house. After a few minutes one of the officers came over (I was still at my neighbor's house) and said that there was no one in the house. I asked him if any of the windows were unlocked or if the back door was open and they assured me that everything was locked up. I told the officers that if everything was still locked up there was no way for him to leave the house, so he must still be in there. They went back and searched again. This time they found him hiding in a bedroom closet. The officers took Mr. Ex away once again and I finally went to work.

Later that evening as I was getting ready for bed, the Lord spoke to me again and directed me to look in the closet where Mr. Ex had been found. When I looked inside the closet, there carefully hidden under some linens was a brand new shiny hunting knife still in its sheath. I knew then that Mr. Ex had not come to "talk," and I gave God thanks for yet another miraculous deliverance. Sometimes the Lord has to show you exactly what He brought you out of. Can I get an "Amen" somebody?

After that episode, I started carrying my own knife, a butcher knife that I swiped from the kitchen. When I would leave my house I would peek out first, check under the car, and look periodically over both shoulders until I got in the car. Once in the car, I would check the rear and side view mirrors to make sure Mr. Ex was nowhere in sight before pulling off. I followed the same procedures when leaving the car. One day as I was about to leave the house I headed into the kitchen to get the knife (I still used it for cooking purposes, you know) when the Lord spoke to me again. He told me that the butcher knife was not the kind of weapon He wanted me to use. He told me to read and memorize Psalm 91 and this would be my weapon. Whenever I was afraid I was to rehearse this passage of scripture. So instead of carrying the knife, I began to carry His Word.

I wore that passage of scripture out! There were many times when I was afraid, and I was still very much in fear of losing my life. At various times, Mr. Ex would show up at church and it used to terrify me. I would stay as far away from him as possible and stick close to a group of people in hopes that he would not try anything with other people around.

One particular weekend, my best friend Faith, (who I'll refer to as my "Faithful Witness"—I'll explain later), told me that she heard her mother in her room praying and calling out my name. When she asked her mother about it, her mother told her that the Lord had led her to pray for my protection. Then Faith, my faithful witness, had a dream that Mr. Ex showed up with a gun to kill me at the church. As she was telling me about the dream I had a horrible feeling that Mr. Ex was going to be at church. Sure enough the next day when I went to church he was there.

I had to sing a solo that day and I was absolutely terrified. I was struggling with whether or not to sing with the choir at all. I prayed and said, "Lord, I feel like an open target, but I'm going to go up there. I place my life in your hands." I was terrified, but I went up, looked out into the congregation, closed my eyes, and sang my heart out. When I was finished and went back to my seat I knew that the Lord had done something. After the service Mr. Ex came up to me and for the first time I didn't run. He didn't say a word. He simply handed me a small piece of paper that said, "I'm sorry for what I've done to our lives." That was it. There was no more fear. I knew that he could not harm me even if he wanted to. From that day forward I was free... at least from *that* kind of fear.

4

justsay**yes!**

I was now past the physical fear and torment of being stalked by Mr. Ex, but there was another lesson in trust that I had to learn. This one was much more difficult. Have you ever been through a season of brokenness? If you have, I'm sure that you will agree that being broken is not a pleasant experience. I went through a major season of brokenness, and let me tell you what the object of the lesson was: for me to say 'yes' to whatever God wanted.

Soon after I separated from Mr. Ex, some of my family members began to pressure me into filing for divorce. Although I had not shared with them the full extent of the abuse that I had endured, they knew enough about some of what I had gone through to come to the conclusion that there could be no way that I would be thinking of getting back together with Mr. Ex. I was reluctant to file for a divorce at that time, not necessarily because I felt that Mr. Ex and I would get back together, but more so because everything was still so fresh and the thought of dealing with the whole legal aspect of terminating the marriage was a bit overwhelming at the time.

One day I came home to find a family member sitting in the living room with an attorney who had been invited to the house specifically for the purpose of convincing me to get divorce proceedings started. I yielded to the pressure of the moment and began proceedings to file for a legal separation (which I was told had to precede a filing for divorce). I reasoned that this was the best thing to do since, in my mind, reconciliation was out of the question. According to the attorney I would have to wait two years after the initial separation before I could start the actual divorce proceedings. It just so happened that during this time of separation, I also separated from my old church.

It was in January of 1992 when I left my old church and became a member of another church. This new church had a doctrine that forbade remarriage under any circumstance except the death of a spouse. When I became a member I placed myself under the authority of that pastor and consequently under that doctrine. This was a completely new doctrine to me, much different from what I had experienced at my former church. Not long after I had separated from Mr. Ex, there were people from my former church encouraging me to remarry. I was still reeling from the whole experience and was not in any hurry to think about marriage. Besides that, even though I was separated, I was still legally married, and so I did not consider myself a candidate for remarriage.

I found myself in an interesting predicament: I was in the waiting period preparing to file for divorce, in a church that taught that you should not get divorced, and if you did get divorced, you could not remarry (while your former spouse was alive). I struggled with the doctrine of this new church, but since I was a member I decided to abide by the teachings of that local body and made up my mind to remain single for the rest of my life. I believed that other than reconciliation, or the untimely demise of Mr. Ex, singleness was my only other option.

The decision to remain single was not an easy decision for me to make. After all, I was still in my early twenties and I expected to have my whole life ahead of me. Initially, I felt cheated, and I went through a period where I was really angry with God. I felt that God had not given me information that He knew would have altered the course of my life, and consequently, the choice of a husband. At the time I married Mr. Ex I did not know anything about "the will of God." I did not know that there was such a thing as God having a plan for my life. I did not know that you could ask God for direction and He would "make your path straight." Even though I had been a believer for a while before I got married, I had not been taught much about scriptural principles. When I got married, as far as I knew, I was doing something that was right and good. But, as I mentioned earlier, my lack of information caused me to make a foolish choice.

As a matter of fact, it wasn't until I visited a church one night in 1991 (two years after I had been separated) and heard a message preached from Proverbs 19:21 ("Many are the plans in a man's heart, but it is the LORD's purpose that prevails.") that I discovered such a concept as "God's will for my life" existed. After hearing that message, I left the church and sat in my car, unable to move. I was so struck with the realization that God actually had a specific plan and direction for my life, that it blew my mind! Among other things, that meant that God had something to say about whether or not I should marry, and if so, who and when. That's when I got angry.

I wondered why God did not allow me to learn this *before* I met Mr. Ex. I ranted and raved about it for several weeks, but eventually, the same thing that caused me to start ranting in the first place was the very thing that calmed me down—the will of God. I came to realize that since God had a plan for my life, His plan was still in effect, and somehow, He was going to cause all of my trouble to "work together for good."

In the meantime, I was in a state of limbo: not single, not divorced, somewhat anxious about getting divorced, and believing that even if I did divorce I could not remarry. To confuse matters, every now and then different people would tell me that they had seen Mr. Ex and how he "looked" like he had changed and how different he seemed. They all encouraged me to give him another chance. That was the most offensive thing anyone could have said to me at that time. I told one person that God would have to come down from heaven Himself and tell me that's what He wanted in order for reconciliation to happen. Well, why did I say that? I did not know it then, but that very statement would prove to be my test.

In the midst of all of this input from other people, Mr. Ex was putting in his "three" cents too. I had moved from where I used to live, but Mr. Ex did not know that I had moved and he was still sending mail to my old address. Because I knew the people that had moved into my old house I received some of his correspondence. I received cards from him telling me how he had rededicated his life to God and how he was now a "man of faith." Oh, and by the way, he even quoted scriptures to support his claims. At first, I totally dismissed them as a ploy on his part, but then eventually, because of the things he was saying and because of his persistence, I started to take note. It all sounded really good; so good, in fact that even Faith, my faithful witness—who was totally against any reconciliation—was being swayed by his words. Even *she* was telling me that maybe I should give him another chance! Believe me, his words had to have been pretty convincing for her to say that knowing all that I had been through. I determined that I would believe nothing Mr. Ex said without some real proof of his change, and that I would watch what he did over time. Remember what I said in the first chapter concerning time's big mouth? If you allow it to, it will tell you everything you need to know.

In the meantime, as all of this was taking place, the Lord was still dealing with me one-on-one. Charles Stanley, a well-known Pastor-Teacher, was doing a series at that time on brokenness. He spoke specifically about how God will break you in that very area that you don't want Him to touch. The area that I did not want God to touch was the possibility of being reconciled with Mr. Ex. Well, the Lord worked me over, and won. It didn't happen overnight, but it did happen as He taught me how to trust Him and believe that His plans for me were good and not evil. By the time He was finished with me, I was able to say, "Lord, I don't want this reconciliation, but if you want this for me, then my answer is 'Yes'."

I was yielded that much to God, but in spite of all of the encouragement to reconcile that I received, whenever I thought about Mr. Ex I got a very uneasy feeling in the pit of my stomach. The sense I had was that things were still not all right where he was concerned. I believed that if God was going to *miraculously* bring us back together, I would have to get past that feeling somehow. I decided that my only course of action was to seek the Lord to find out if there was any basis for my uneasiness.

I completed a three-day fast—no food or water—with three specific prayer requests in mind: "Lord, I want you to show me what's going on in Mr. Ex's life; I want to know if he is sincere about what he has been saying; and I want to know everything that has happened from the time we split up until now. Good or bad, I want to know everything." That was my prayer and focus for three days.

From the time I first started to hear from Mr. Ex I began having dreams about him a lot. The dreams were always the same: Mr. Ex would be pursuing me, trying to win me back. He would *look* fine and there were times when other people in the dream were telling me that he had changed. But always in each dream, just as he would get close to me and I was beginning to waver in his favor, I would see that he had not changed and that he was trying to destroy me. Always at that point in the dream, he would be within close range but some invisible force would always kill him. Sometimes it would seem that he had been shot, though I would never hear a shot or see who shot him. He was always struck by something that I could never see. At the time I did not fully understand the dreams, but I would always remember them. Anyway, let's get back to my prayer requests.

About two weeks after I completed the fast and seeking God's face concerning Mr. Ex's true intentions, the Lord answered my prayers in a most amazing way. It was February of 1993, and I was expecting to receive the usual seasonal (Valentine's Day) card from Mr. Ex, but I did not. I had never responded to any of his cards. I figured if he was on a mission from God as he claimed, whether he heard from me or not should not have affected what he claimed he was doing (i.e. trying to win me back). He claimed that he would continue to send cards and that he would not give up. Well, so much for that claim.

A few days after Valentine's Day, I received a phone call one evening from a young lady I knew from my old church. She told me that one of Mr. Ex's relatives (who lived out of state) wanted me to call him. The relative never gave her the reason why he wanted me to call, but only left his phone number and asked that I get in touch with him right away. I had met this relative at least once before, but I did not really know him at all so this was quite unusual. I didn't have a clue what he wanted. I was surprised, but I didn't make any real connection between this call and my prayer request.

When I called him the next day, he asked me about something so trivial that it was absurd. I wondered why on earth he would want me to call him long distance just to ask me such a simple question. But then, without my asking any questions, he began to tell me all about Mr. Ex. He told me *everything* that had happened from the time we had been separated until that present day. He told me how Mr. Ex had moved to the same state he was living in after telling his family how I threw him out (he never told them about his abuse). He told me of how Mr. Ex had moved in with a woman and later married her (the fact that we were still legally married did not deter him). He told me how Mr. Ex had gotten this woman pregnant twice, and on both occasions he purposely abused the woman in such a way that she lost both babies, nearly dying the second time. He told me of how the woman left Mr. Ex and literally had to run for her life and change jobs in order to get away from his threats of shooting her. This news really shocked me because it made me realize how wicked Mr. Ex's behavior really was. I say this, not only because of the abuse. I'll explain.

In one of his former correspondences, Mr. Ex told me that after we separated he was in such a bad state of mind that he met and married someone else. He told me that while he was with this woman the Lord was telling him that he should be reconciled with me. He told me of how the woman had been expecting his child, but here's the kicker: he told me that the *Lord* took the baby's life in order to show him that the relationship he had with the woman was not approved by Him. This is how utterly wicked his actions were that not only would he marry another woman (while he was still married) and abuse her, but that he would intentionally cause the miscarriage of two innocent babies, nearly killing the mother, and then say that God did it!

But, that was not all. The relative went on to tell me that after that, Mr. Ex seduced a young girl in the church he was attending and convinced her to leave her mother's home and move in with him. The girl, who had been active in her church choir, was approached by some of the elders in the church who told her that she would either have to leave the choir or leave Mr. Ex alone (apparently, it was known that he was married). The girl decided to leave the choir and went with Mr. Ex. The relative told me how they had gone to a church convention together, and on the way back home, they were involved in a car accident that totaled the car that they were driving. The relative said that he asked Mr. Ex if he believed that God was warning him about his lifestyle. He said that Mr. Ex responded that there was nothing wrong with what he was doing. When the relative stated that Mr. Ex acted as if he thought he was invincible, Mr. Ex stated, matter-of-factly, that he was.

There were other appalling details but I think you get the picture. All of this was taking place in Mr. Ex's life during the time he was sending me his scripture-filled cards and letters. My prayer request had been answered in full. I thanked the relative for the information, said good-bye and that was the last time we spoke. I realized that God had again, as in times past, most graciously spared me from grave danger. Eventually, I came to realize that it was not reconciliation that God had in mind, but obedience on my part to His will, whatever it might be.

Do you remember the story of Abraham's sacrifice of Isaac? When the Lord told Abraham that he was to sacrifice his only son, it was the hardest thing for him to do, but he said yes to the Lord. As he moved in obedience, God showed Abraham that the act— the killing of his son—was the outward demonstration of the commitment to obedience that had already taken place in his heart, and that was really all that God wanted.

In my case, I thought that the Lord was leading me towards reconciliation, which for me was the hardest sacrifice I could have made at that time. Thankfully, as was the case with Abraham, my heart's commitment to obedience was really what God was after. The mission had been accomplished: I had been broken to the point of being willing to say "yes" to God, no matter what He wanted.

5

theabigail**syndrome**

I was now broken and yielded, but was I content? Apparently not. I thought I was, but for the remainder of the year (1993) the Lord taught me one recurring lesson: you are complete in Him (Colossians 2:10). It was drilled into me. Everywhere I went I heard the same message: in church, on the car radio, in my personal study. Complete in Him. *Complete* in Him. *Complete in Him!* I was still in the same church, under the same doctrine, and now with the possibility of reconciliation completely out the window, I had to really deal with the prospect of singleness for the rest of my life. I came to realize that no matter what happened, God was enough to fill any void in my life. Once I accepted the fact that God was enough, I experienced tremendous peace, and I knew that if singleness had to be my lot in life I would be all right. It was important for God to bring me to the point where I was able to say that *and* mean it. To say that I was resigned to remaining single for the rest of my life was one thing; to say that I would remain single for the rest of my life and be satisfied was another.

Initially it was hard for me to think of having to remain single forever, especially when I knew Mr. Ex was out there having relationships. It didn't seem fair. But God was showing me that He was enough. God could love me enough; He could take care of me; He could satisfy my soul. I began to realize that God really loved me and that He wanted the very best for me—even more than I wanted it for myself.

I threw myself full force into ministry and His word became the most important thing to me. I was in Bible school on Mondays and Tuesdays; Bible study and prayer meeting on Wednesdays; young women's fellowship on Thursdays; Bible study on Friday; whatever church related function was going on Saturday; Sunday school and morning worship service on Sunday—sometimes capping the day off with an "if it's all night, it's all right" evening service. This went on for some time, and in the midst of my learning completeness in Him, I also learned about balancing my time and energy. Before I wore myself out completely, I eventually cut down on the all week church attendance. Trust. Brokenness. Completeness. Balance. What else was there for me to learn? A whole lot more.

I was involved in ministry. I was learning what my gifts were, and how to use them. Our church had an annual youth and teen camp every summer, and towards the latter part of 1993 the Lord laid on my heart to go to camp the following year. By the summer of 1994, around the time when some missionaries from my church were going to Kenya, for some reason I started wondering about Kenya. I started praying about whether or not the Lord wanted me to go to Kenya. As I was wondering and praying about going, the Lord led me back to a book that I had read concerning missions. There was a certain portion of text that I remembered reading about ways to discern the Lord's will. Simply stated it asked, "Have you done the last thing that the Lord told you to do." As I read it, I immediately remembered how the Lord had put going to teen camp on my heart the previous year and I knew that this was what I was supposed to do. So, in August of 1994, off I went to youth and teen camp to serve as a teen counselor.

The Lord accomplished a lot for me while I was there for those two weeks that summer. I was there to counsel the teens, but I was the one who ended up being counseled the most. The Lord began to show me things about myself. He began to confirm the gifts and talents that He had invested in me. By the time I went back home, many prayer requests that I made prior to leaving had been answered. I had a clearer picture of what my gifts were, and I had a clearer sense of direction concerning God's will for my life.

Not long after I came back from camp, I was in my room exercising one night and even though I was moving around a lot, I was focused and prayerful in thought. As my thoughts traveled from one area of my life to the next, the thought of marriage resurfaced. I had not been thinking much about marriage for a while. Whenever my friends and I got together and the conversation turned to men and relationships with them (as it did so often), my response was always the same: "I'm dead to that." For all intents and purposes, I really was dead to it. I was not looking for a relationship, not giving it a whole lot of thought, not entertaining any advances, turning down opportunities to meet guys who were interested in a relationship, and so on. But that evening marriage came to mind. Actually, it wasn't marriage, per se, but what I remember thinking about was the whole scenario with Mr. Ex. I was reviewing all the changes I had gone through in trusting the Lord for my safety and being open to the will of God and learning to be content in the state that I was in. I thought about the different stages I had gone through thinking that I would be reconciled with Mr. Ex and how that whole scenario had ended. In my thoughts I asked one simple question: "What now?" As quickly as the thought entered my mind, the response came back in one word that flashed in my mind: *Abigail.*

I was sure I had read about Abigail at some point in my Christian life, but I was not familiar with her story. Curiosity got the best of me, so I stopped exercising, got my Bible, and tried to find any related passages. I found one in I Samuel 25. It told of Abigail and her relationship with her husband Nabal. The story was vaguely familiar, and as I read the story I felt a strange connection with Abigail. I began to notice similarities between Abigail and myself. She was also married to a wicked fool who had no regard for God or His people. I couldn't help wondering why she married him in the first place since she was described as a wise and discerning woman. It occurred to me that this story was related to marriage in some way, but I wasn't sure how it specifically related to me. I made a note in my journal about it and pushed it to the back of my mind with really not much more than a mental shrug. That's when, what I call, the "Abigail syndrome" started.

For months after, the passage of scripture in I Samuel chapter 25 kept coming to mind. It was bombarding my thoughts! I began to wonder why this passage of scripture kept coming to my mind. Was it coming from God, the devil, or me? I was annoyed because I didn't understand what the passage meant. I kept asking God what significance, if any, the passage had for me. It became so much of a burden to me that I decided to enter again into a time of fasting and seek God's face about it. I did not believe that the Lord would allow me to be deceived, especially now that I had learned to seek His will and not my own. I believed that if this was a trick of the enemy, or something of my own doing, God would expose it to me. He did say that His sheep hear *His* voice (John 10:27). Once again my prayer was focused: I prayed that God would let me know what significance this passage had for me and that He would confirm His will for me through His word. Even more specifically, I asked God to let me know if He was speaking to me directly about marriage.

During and after the time of fasting I continued to pray earnestly. Every day during my lunch break and each evening I would meet with the Lord and pray specifically about this Abigail thing (as I later referred to it). As I would sit quietly, different scriptures would come to mind (I Corinthians 2:9, 10; Psalm 84:11; Jeremiah 33:3; the latter portion of Hebrews 11:6; John 15:7; Proverbs 3:5,6; Psalm 37 to name a few). I would look up the scriptures and write them down. It seemed that scripture after scripture confirmed that this whole Abigail scenario was indeed a word from the Lord for me. But I still was not convinced, and I still wasn't sure what it all meant. Everywhere I went someone would reference a scripture that would seem to be confirmation. I would hear the same scriptures referenced by friends, on radio broadcasts, during Bible study, in Bible school; I even heard many references specifically about Abigail. Granted, some of the scriptures were fairly well known, but one scripture in particular really grabbed my attention because it was one I had never heard before. This particular verse—found in Isaiah 42:9—talked about how God will show you things that He's going to do *before* He does them.

In spite of all of this, I still could not bring myself to accept that God was speaking to me concerning marriage. I had become so comfortable in my "singleness" and had become so used to the idea of not being able to remarry (because of the doctrinal teaching I was under) that the thought of God speaking to me about marriage was a little scary and definitely unbelievable.

One night in particular stands out in my memory. It was November 1, 1994, a Tuesday night. That night Faith (the Faithful Witness) and I were coming home from church and she was sharing with me how God was certainly leading her to the missions field. On my way home, after dropping Faith off, I pondered the things she had told me and I marveled at how God was working in her life. By the time I got home I had a very unsettling sort of feeling that gave me the distinct impression that the Lord wanted my undivided attention. I went into my room, sat on the edge of my bed and said, in effect, "Lord, I'm listening." Then I knelt down and repeated the phrase. Again, Abigail came to mind. I was annoyed and frustrated at this point. I shook my head and thought, "No. This has got to be me!" I thought, "Lord, I've already read about that." At the same time, without consciously thinking I reached for my Bible. I had been reading through the book of Jeremiah and I had a bookmark in the place where I had stopped reading, but as I opened my Bible, it did not open to where the bookmark was as it normally did, but instead it opened directly to the book of I Samuel chapter 25. The only thing that was missing was the theme song from the Twilight Zone! Bookmark or no bookmark, I just could not get away from that passage of scripture!

As time wore on, my struggle with the Abigail syndrome

continued and I continued in prayer. A few weeks later, on November 28, 1994, I reached a turning point. I was parked at one of my usual lunch-n-pray spots and I was praying about the whole Abigail-marriage thing. I still could not bring myself to believe that God was speaking to me about marriage, even though the scriptures I read and heard seemed to confirm that. It was a bit frightening to me to think that God was really telling me about His future plans. I prayed about it, and then one by one I began to review some of the scriptures that the Lord had given me. By the time I was finished reading, it was as if the Lord had given me a dollop of faith just to believe that He indeed was speaking to me concerning marriage and that He had given me a glimpse of what He had planned for me in the future.

I prayed and told the Lord that if this was His will then I accepted it. I began to cry, not from joy about the prospect of being married again, but just because of the awesomeness of God sharing with me His future plans. I also cried a little out of selfishness that someone else, namely a husband, might disrupt this intimate relationship that had developed between God and me. I had really gotten used to it being just God and me.

As you may have gathered by now, I did keep a journal of these significant events which has helped me to be exact about the dates. However, there's another special reason why I remember the date November 28, 1994 so well. In the earlier months when the Lord first pointed out the story of Abigail to me, I sat in my room one evening pondering the Abigail story. As I thought about the wickedness of Nabal, I felt very grieved to think that I was still legally married to a man who I considered to be even more wicked. I began to express my feelings to God. I told him that I did not want to be bound to a man that was so wicked and I wondered if I would ever be free of him. I felt a certain stigma knowing that I was bound to someone who I did not want to be associated with. As I sat there, a passage of scripture came to mind concerning the Year of Jubilee. I was not familiar with this passage either so I looked it up. As I read, I was led to a cross reference that caught my attention. It spoke of the seventh year being the year when slaves were released, and I couldn't help wondering if the Lord was speaking to me about being released from Mr. Ex. There seemed to be something significant about the number seven in this passage. I meditated on the phrase "the seventh year" and what that could possibly mean. If the Lord was speaking to me about future things, did this mean that seven years from the time Mr. Ex and I were separated I would be released? That would mean that it would happen in 1996. Perhaps it meant seven years from the time we were married. Since I really didn't know what to make of it, I jotted it down in my journal and left it alone.

Throughout the entire Abigail episode, in my prayers I had been asking for some tangible form of confirmation. I know it's not good to ask for signs, but that's basically what I was asking for. I just wanted to be sure that I was in the Lord's perfect will. On the day of my turning point, after I had finished praying and was reversing the car to drive back to the office, the Lord spoke to me again and said, "Now you'll get your confirmation." It was so clear a message that I actually laughed out loud. Simultaneously, as the Lord was speaking to me, that day's date—November, 28, 1994—flashed in my mind. I promised myself that I would look at that date on the calendar as soon as I got back to the office to see if there was anything significant about it. When I got back to the office, I did just that, but on a strange impulse, I counted back seven years, and much to my surprise discovered that it had been exactly seven years to the day that I had been married. I need you to understand just how significant that was for me. I had long since thrown away everything I could get my hands on that reminded me of the wedding day—all the videos, mementos, pictures, etc.—everything that I could find, and for many years I could not even remember the date I got married. For me, this was a very powerful confirmation.

What I learned from that experience was that faith many times precedes confirmation. When you think about it, something has to be set in order before it is confirmed, doesn't it? You have to make the appointment before it is confirmed. My faith set the appointment, and God used the significance of that date and the "seventh year" to confirm it! I had accepted the fact that God had marriage in store for me. What I didn't know was who, where, or when. I thought I had the 'how' pretty much figured out (more on that later). For now, the wait (and the watch) was on.

6

stillin**school**

Even with all that had happened, in the days and months to come, I found myself doubtful at times. Whenever I became doubtful, I would somehow be reminded of Abraham and how God made a seemingly impossible promise to him. The scripture says that Abraham believed God and he did not stagger at God's promise, unlike me who did a whole lot of staggering! Many times I felt that Abraham and I didn't have that much in common as far as faith was concerned. Here's one example.

Very early on the morning of December 26, 1994, I woke up in a panic. I woke up feeling extremely discouraged about the whole Abigail thing (yes, that again). I was thinking that I had fooled myself into believing something that wasn't true, and that there was no significance in the "seventh year" date. I woke up convinced that my actual marriage date was November 27, 1988. I was in a state of total confusion! I jumped up and started to search for anything that might prove me right. I really don't know what I had expected to find since I had long since thrown out every reminder of the marriage that I could get my hands on. Surprisingly enough I found a memento from the wedding reception that had the date printed on it. There it was in bold silver print *November 28, 1987* which meant that the seventh year confirmation had indeed been significant. I went back to bed feeling relieved that I was not going completely insane, but when I woke up later that morning I was still troubled.

As I mentioned earlier, I had been reading through the book of Jeremiah, but this morning, the Lord led me to read Genesis 15. I started reading and read through to Chapter 18. There was a verse of scripture that had been ringing in my head since the time I woke up and, lo and behold, as I read through these chapters I ran right into it! It's the verse where the Lord asks, "Is there anything too hard for me?" It seemed as if the Lord was asking me the same question. After I finished reading in Genesis, I went back to the place where I had left off in Jeremiah, chapter 32. As I read down to verse 17, there it was again, "Is anything too hard for the Lord?", and again in verse 27, "Behold, I am the Lord, the God of all flesh; is anything too hard for me?" Three times in one morning in two separate passages of scripture was enough convincing for me. My mind was set at ease again... at least for the time being.

I had a lot to learn about faith and holding onto the promise of God. There were still a lot of other things I had to learn as well such as understanding that a lot of times when the Lord speaks to us and shows us something that He has planned for us, His timeline is much different than ours. When I finally accepted the idea of being married again I messed up in a couple of ways. For one thing, I had a "right now" spirit. I thought that if God had shown me this thing "now," He's going to do this thing "now." Wrong! I had to learn that God's timing is not ours and there is always something greater that He is teaching us than what we think. One thing you can be sure of, complete trust in Him is always part of the curriculum: it's a required part of every course.

Another mistake I made was in "leaning to my own understanding." While I had accepted the idea of being married again, I was still holding on to the same doctrine of no remarriage unless the former spouse dies. So what did I do? I waited for Mr. Ex to die. As funny (or maybe not as funny) as it sounds, I did not wish Mr. Ex any harm, but because I was so deeply entrenched in the doctrine of no divorce and subsequent remarriage, that was the only way my finite little mind could comprehend this whole thing coming to be. It was only logical, right? If I could not remarry unless my former spouse was dead, and if God had shown and told me that His will for me was to be married again, the only logical conclusion I could reach was that Mr. Ex must die. It made perfect sense to me! Consequently, for a long time I waited to hear the news of his untimely demise, and when I say "waiting," I mean *literally* waiting. There were times when the phone would ring and I would wonder, "Is this it?" (I really was a bit of a basket case.) This is an example of what happens when we try to figure things out on our own. I was trusting God. The problem was that I was trusting God for the wrong thing, and He wasn't about to let me get away with that.

It all came to a head one day when I got a letter from Mr. Ex in the mail. The letter was actually from Mr. Ex's live-in girlfriend (the same person the relative told me about). She wrote the letter as if Mr. Ex was speaking, but I knew Mr. Ex well enough to know that this was not his writing or speaking style. She was basically prompting me to go ahead and file for divorce so that Mr. Ex could marry her, the mother of his recently newborn son. Newborn son! That hit a nerve for me... a very painful one. Don't get me wrong,

I did not wish that it was me in her place or anything like that, but it just didn't seem fair! Here I was trying to live right and "wait patiently on the Lord" (well, as patiently as I knew how), and there he was, living just as wickedly as ever, prospering and being blessed! I understood then what Asaph went through when he penned the 73rd Psalm.

After I read the letter, the first opportunity I had to be completely alone, I fell prostrate on the floor and cried out to God. I was frustrated, having been separated and in a state of limbo for what was then six years, and it had been nearly a year since I had accepted the promise. Nothing had ever come of the legal separation because after I became a member of the new church, there never was a filing for divorce. I was still somewhere between living in matrimony and being unmarried. I didn't know what category I fit into. One of the things I came to hate was filling out forms that asked about my marital status. I never knew what to put!

The feeling of limbo coupled with the additional frustration of waiting for the vision of marriage to become a reality—a critical step for me being the news of Mr. Ex's death only to hear news of him prospering—was a bit too much for me. I wailed, rolled around, and everything in between. I just couldn't understand what God was doing. How could the wicked (i.e. Mr. Ex) prosper like that when the scriptures said that the wicked would surely be cut off? It was then that the Holy Spirit began to deal with my heart about forgiveness. He reminded me of times before when I said I had completely forgiven Mr. Ex. I thought I had, but with the emphasis He placed on *complete* forgiveness, I had to pause and think about it again. While I paused He asked me some more questions: how could I have completely forgiven Mr. Ex and still be waiting for his death? Was that forgiveness?

The answer was simple. If I had truly forgiven Mr. Ex I would not be waiting to hear of something bad happening to him. The challenge, the test, and the lesson for me this time was forgiveness: complete and total forgiveness. I repented right then and there and asked God to forgive me. I realized that it really isn't God's will that any should perish, but that all should come to repentance, even the wicked, and yes... even Mr. Ex. When I got up off the floor I had been delivered—I had passed my test—but I still didn't understand how this vision of marriage would come to pass, especially now that the death thing was out.

takeanother**look**

Before I go any further, I must fill in a very important piece of this puzzle. Something happened that I later realized was going to be a critical component in the realization of my vision. I had been working for the same company for seven years by this time, and during this time I met a lady named Mary.

Mary and I shared an office space for nearly four years and we became friends. Both of us had been married and at the beginning of our friendship, both of us were separated. Naturally, during the course of our friendship, we shared some of our experiences. Mary was also a Christian and she belonged to a church that taught that you could remarry after divorce. During that time, I was still a member of the church that taught no remarriage unless your former spouse dies. I was not only a member, but I had become a diehard, staunch, dogmatic believer of this teaching.

Previously, I had been a member of a church where teaching had not been a primary focus. When I became a member of this church that was very teaching oriented, I soaked up and assimilated every bit of teaching that was presented. Initially, I was not yet mature enough spiritually to "eat the fish and get rid of the bones," so I ate the whole fish, bones and all! I didn't start choking until I was faced with questions that I could not answer using the same dogmatic scriptures that I had been taught. Mary was the person that caused the first bone to get stuck in my throat.

As we worked together, Mary would talk to me about the possibility of her getting divorced and perhaps one day remarrying. She was in a position where she did not want to be divorced but her spouse (who was an unbeliever) did. Whenever the subject of remarriage came up, though our discussions were always friendly, my response was always the same: no can do! What I said to her in effect was that it didn't matter how her divorce came about; it didn't matter what the circumstances were that led to her divorce; it did not matter if there was any change of behavior; or if the possibility of reconciliation existed. The only thing that mattered was that if she got divorced, she could not remarry as long as her spouse was still alive. Of course, I always supported what I was saying with convenient scriptural references. I was very well versed in the dogma, but I found that as Mary asked more and more specific questions and posed various scenarios from her own experience, my dogmatic scriptures and answers were not fully answering her questions. I was beginning to choke on the bones.

One day, Mary and I got into our usual discussion concerning divorce and remarriage. There was one specific passage that Mary mentioned that referred to the situation in which an unbelieving mate wants to divorce the mate who has become a believer. This was one of Mary's personal scenarios. Normally I would have quickly responded with the usual answer, but on that particular day I paused to think about the question and about my answer before I spoke. I had to admit to myself that my answer would have been superficial at best and would not have reached the heart of the issue. I told

Mary that I would do some studying and get back to her with an answer.

I went home and began my research. My intention was to find appropriate scriptures that would refute the possibility of remarriage after divorce (while the former spouse is still living). So I set about my task. My strategy was to use an exhaustive concordance to make a list of every scripture that dealt with divorce and remarriage in both the Old and New Testaments and then systematically study each scripture, looking at the audience, the context, and any questions raised and being answered in each passage. As I began making my list, I found that I could not limit the subject of study to only divorce and remarriage, but that I had to include all the references on marriage as well since that was where it all began. My list was long, but I was determined to find the answers.

As I began my study, much to my surprise, instead of finding more scriptures to support my stance, I began to find scriptures that seemed to contradict what I believed. This threw me for a loop! How could this be? Fortunately, I had three premises when I began my study: 1) God does not lie; 2) God does not change; and 3) God's word is true. With these three premises in mind I was forced to humble myself and admit that while I thought I was a fairly (*ahem*) skilled expositor on the scriptures concerning remarriage (yes, I am being facetious), I really didn't have a clue. I had to start all over from scratch. I had to forget about everything I thought I knew, and ask the Lord to teach me His perspective. Now I was in a place and mindset to be taught. It was as if the Lord had been waiting for me to reach this point so that He could teach me something.

The scriptures started to come together and my understanding gradually became clearer and clearer. I meditated daily on whatever passage I was studying, sometimes for weeks at a time. My goal was now the truth: whatever the truth was, that's what I wanted to know. I am a witness that if you want to know God's perspective on a matter, and you earnestly, diligently, prayerfully and open-mindedly search the scriptures and meditate on them, God will give you understanding. The scriptures began to open up to me. I would fall asleep meditating on a particular passage and sometimes I would wake up in the middle of the night with a fresh new perspective that I had not seen before.

I kept notes during my study, and before long I had a small booklet of related information. I shared with Mary only that I was still studying, but I was reluctant to tackle her question again until I was certain that I had an understanding of the truth and that I would be able to clearly articulate what I had learned. I did not realize it until I was finished that my study took nearly two years to complete (I finished in October of 1996). When I was finished, I compiled my notes into a story form that related primarily to the issues and questions that Mary had been asking me about. I shared the information with her, beginning first with an apology for the responses I had given her previously.

Having come to a new understanding of the Biblical perspective on marriage, divorce, and remarriage, I began to look at my own situation differently. I had transitioned from being repulsed at the thought of being reconciled, to being open to the possibility of reconciliation if that's what God wanted (but God forbid), to having no thoughts or plans of ever remarrying, to being content to be perpetually single, to struggling with but finally accepting the idea that marriage would be a part of my future after all (but only after the death of my spouse), to not knowing how on earth remarriage would happen since it was apparent that I was wrong to sit and wait for my spouse to croak (and it didn't appear that he would be croaking any time soon anyway).

Even though I had reached a point after studying the scriptures where it was clear that I could be divorced and remarry, I still did not want to make any hasty moves. I decided to do what the words of a song (written by Carol Antrom) says, "I'll just stand still until Your will is clear to me." This did not mean that I became complacent. It meant that I believed that God had given me a clear direction for my future and that I did not need to be overly concerned with *how* His plan was going to be accomplished. I could use the resources available to me to make whatever decisions needed to be made when I needed to make them, but I did not have to run after the vision; I only had to wait for it to come to pass as God had promised.

In March of 1995, the words of another passage of scripture kept coming to mind that spoke of waiting for the vision that God gives to come to fruition. This was definitely a verse that I had heard before, but I did not know where it was located. I made a mental note to look up the location (chapter and verse) of the scripture, but someone else beat me to it. One night, while I was in class at Bible school, one of the teachers chose the text from Habakkuk 2:1-4 as his opening text, and there in verse 3 was the scripture that had been coming to mind: "For the vision is yet for the appointed time; it hastens toward the goal, and it will not fail. Though it tarries, wait for it; for it will certainly come, it will not delay." When I studied that scripture (Habakkuk 2:3) in the Hebrew language, it spoke of a very specific time that had been predetermined for the vision to be realized. It also gave the assurance that 1) the vision would not turn out to be a lie; 2) that it would certainly happen; and 3) when it did begin to happen, it would unfold very quickly. So there I was in a state of limbo holding onto a vision that had been given to me concerning marriage, but now with a whole new perspective. I had to go back to square one, put aside all of my notions of how I thought things were supposed to happen, and find out from God what He had in mind.

As I waited and as time passed, I became increasingly frustrated with the feeling of being in limbo. About a year or so after we had been separated, Mr. Ex told me that he would be filing for divorce. (I had not mentioned to him that I was already planning to file for divorce in another year. I figured, let him pay for it!) Since I had extremely little contact with him and had not received any paperwork I did not know if he had started proceedings for divorce or not, so I decided to find out.

In December of 1996, a couple months after finishing my study, I sent Mr. Ex a simple note asking him if he had filed for divorce. He responded that he had not filed because he had been hoping that we would get back together. (Can you believe it?) He was prepared to abandon the woman he had been living with for over three years (who by that time had two sons with him), and be reconciled with me. I knew this was not going to happen.

By this time, we had been separated for eight years and during this time getting a divorce was not on the top of my priority list. There had been no need to rush. When we first separated, neither reconciliation, nor divorce and remarriage were appealing to me. I didn't want to make any rash decisions or hasty moves so I focused my attention on my personal healing and growth. After over three years of separation I became a part of a church that taught that I couldn't remarry anyway, and then later I believed that God was going to smite Mr. Ex. With these things in mind there really had been no reason to press the issue of divorce.

When I responded to Mr. Ex's letter, I did not tell him how absurd I thought his notion of reconciliation was. I had used the eight years of separation to grow as an individual, but based on Mr. Ex's words and actions, it did not seem that he had made any positive changes. If anything, it seemed any changes he had made had been for the worse. Why he thought I would be motivated to be reconciled with him was beyond me, but I didn't tell him that. What I did tell him was that it was time for him to start taking responsibility for his actions and get the help that he knew he needed. I told him that he needed to be the father that his children needed him to be, and to do right by the mother of his children. When he received my letter, he filed for divorce soon thereafter.

His ground for divorce was irretrievable breakdown. When I read that, something in me rose up in indignation. I wanted to scream, "What about the physical abuse, the emotional torment, the pornography, the adultery, the abandonment, the bigamy?" It didn't seem fair that the record should state only "irretrievable breakdown," but I rested in the assurance that God knew the real deal and it is His record that really counts. So after nearly nine years of separation, in 1997, I officially became an unmarried woman. My time of limbo as far as my previous marital status was over.

The subject of divorce and remarriage is unfortunately a divisive one in the Church. But it shouldn't be that way. There are many Christians who find themselves in circumstances where they have become victims of divorce and who live in a state of perpetual condemnation because they have not taken the time to find out what God's perspective is on their situations.

The issues of marriage and divorce are discussed in both the Old and New Testaments. God has set forth boundaries for marriage and for the dissolution of it. Every act of divorce and remarriage does not constitute adultery.

In the Old Testament, God addressed the issue of divorce and remarriage because there were people (i.e. women) who were being exploited by acts of divorce. In those days, a man could divorce his wife for any and every reason. To prevent the divorced woman from living in a state of shame, disgrace, and poverty, God (through Moses) gave instructions to provide such women with a lawful certificate of divorce so that she would be free to marry again (Deuteronomy 24:1-2). God never provides instruction that will cause His people to sin. As such, if you find one act of remarriage in scripture that is not condemned as sin, then you cannot deem *all* acts of remarriage as sin without contradicting scripture.

God never contradicts Himself, He never changes, and He cannot lie. This is why we use scripture to interpret scripture. All scripture, Old and New Testaments, must be in agreement with one another. In the New Testament, Christ does not abolish or disregard the instruction given in Deuteronomy. Instead, He provides further explanation for the need for the certificate of divorce (i.e. the hard-heartedness of men who would divorce their wives for whatever cause suited them). The question was asked, "Can a man divorce (put away) his wife for any and every cause?" Christ's answer was 'No' (Matthew 19:3-9). Not all divorces are lawful in God's eyes.

Paul also addressed the issue in I Corinthians 7. In that chapter, he speaks to three distinct categories: those who are married, those who are unmarried (i.e. divorced or widowed), and those who were never married (virgins). He begins by supporting what Christ has said, and then addresses various scenarios that relate to marriage, divorce, and remarriage. He does not, however, condemn the act of remarriage by a divorced person. Paul clearly states that if a divorced (i.e. unmarried) person remarries, "He [or she] has not sinned" (I Corinthians 7:27,28). These verses, as with any verse in scripture, must be interpreted in light of what has already been said.

Malachi 2:14 is often singled out as a foundation for the position against divorce or to support the position of no remarriage after divorce. But God took the time to let us know in Malachi 2:13-16 that He not only hates divorce, but that He also hates marital unfaithfulness. He calls it dealing "treacherously." Note the various meanings assigned to the word 'treacherous'[1]:

Willful betrayal of fidelity, confidence, or trust
Deliberate breach of faith; calculated violation of trust
Not to be relied on; not dependable or trustworthy
Marked by unforeseen hazards; dangerous or deceptive
Not true to duty or obligation; disloyal
Having no religious faith
Unworthy of faith or trust; unreliable

God has declared that He hates treachery *and* divorce. Which one does He hate more? For some reason, many denominations have decided that God hates the act of divorce more. This is one example of how we allow our own bias and narrow-mindedness to color our interpretation of the scripture. I believe that we would be more effective in combating divorce if we the Church dealt more with the "treacherous" behavior that often leads to divorce, rather than focusing singly on the act of divorce itself.

Christ gave the Church authority—particularly those in leadership—to mediate civil matters among believers (Matthew 18:15-19), including matters concerning marriage and divorce. If the issue is the contemplation of divorce or remarriage, consideration should be given to the grounds that led to divorce or the contemplation of it. Divorce is never a mandate. By that I mean even if a person has grounds for a lawful divorce, that does not mean that a divorce is necessary or the best option. It depends on the situation and the willingness of the couple involved to change in such a way as to promote harmony in their marriage. However, whatever the marital offense, complete forgiveness *is* a mandate (Ephesians 4:31,32). Some marriages can be saved if the couples involved are open to wise and godly counsel and if there is change in destructive behavior and attitudes. We must investigate the option of reconciliation to see if that might be a possibility.

A bad marriage is painful and divorce is overwhelming, sometimes more devastating than death. There are more people than we know walking around in our churches with cheerful façades, but in their souls and spirits they are bruised, battered, and broken. Psalm 42:3 says, "A bruised reed He shall not break..." so why do we have so many people who are *more* broken *because* they are a part of the Church? We must be doing something wrong. People who are being affected by either a bad marriage or a divorce need to be ministered to. Psalm 107:20 says, "He sent his word, and healed them, and delivered them from their destructions." And what better way to find healing than through the word of God. As the scripture says, it is our responsibility to minister to others whenever we have opportunity, *especially* to those who are of the household of faith (Galatians 6:10).

It has been said that there is more divorce in the Church than in the world. This indicates that the Church is failing to effectively provide counsel in the areas of pre-marital and marital instruction. We have the blueprint! We must counsel both the married and the unmarried on how to avoid divorce and experience the blessings of marriage as God had originally intended.

¹ Webster's Revised Unabridged Dictionary (Springfield, Mass.: C. & G. Merriam Company, 1913, 1996, 1998).

8

intransition

God has a way of slowly bringing you to the point where He wants you to be. He very rarely quickly grills you over flaming hot coals (although it may sometimes feel that way). Rotisserie—a nice *slow* roast—seems to be one of His choice methods for making sure you're "well done," and guess who was still on the skewer!

I was now a free woman, both legally and spiritually. As the Bible puts it, I was "not bound." I had been released from my previous marriage, and I knew that I had the freedom to marry again. The question at the tip of my mind now and again was, "*Who* was I supposed to marry?" I had the vision, the promise, the freedom, everything but the "sacrifice." Surely Jehovah Jireh had provided a "Ram" in the thicket for me to bring to the altar, but where on earth was the thicket, and who was the Ram? Was he a tall Ram? Was he a fat Ram? Was he a good looking Ram? Did I mention I didn't know where the thicket was? What do you do when God has promised you a companion but you don't see anyone in sight? You wait. What do you do when you've already been waiting for that companion that God has promised you and you still don't see anyone in sight? You wait some more. You can throw a tantrum, roll on the floor, cry, kick, scream, and even pout if you want to, but when it's all said and done, you still have to wait. But while you're waiting, whether you realize it or not, God is moving you towards the plan that He has in mind. Here's an example of what I mean.

One Sunday morning in the summer of 1994, several missionaries were being commissioned to go to the mission field in Africa. As I sat in my seat the Holy Spirit impressed very strongly within my spirit that I would be leaving that church. I had only been there for about two years at that point, and I had settled in quite nicely. My friend Faith (my Faithful Witness) and I both joined the church at the same time and it seemed from the day we became members, and even a little before then, that God had given us special favor. We were taken under the Pastor's wings and given many, many wonderful opportunities to both grow and serve.

On that particular Sunday, Faith and I sat in our usual spots in the third pew from the front on the right-hand side of the church. After the Holy Spirit had revealed to me that I would be leaving, I turned to her and told her that I would be leaving that church some day. She nodded in response, and after we had both let the thought digest for a few moments, we turned our attention back to the service. Most of the time when the Lord would reveal something to me I would share it at some point with Faith. This is why I refer to her as my "Faithful Witness." I shared these things with her so that I would have someone who could attest to what God had done when He did it. This was one such instance.

As I mentioned earlier, I came to learn that when God tells you something He does not always mean it's going to happen right then and there. Sometimes the wait is lengthy: days, weeks, months, even years! In this particular instance, it would take three more years before God was ready to move me from that church. I often wondered why He would tell me things and then make me wait. But as I mentioned before, I later learned that a requisite for any course God is teaching is trust. One of the best aids that God uses to teach us to trust in Him is time.

Three years after the Lord revealed to me that I would be leaving, I knew it was time to leave. Nothing else was said and there were no reminders given, but when the time came, I knew it. It was as if an internal alarm clock went off letting me know it was time to get up and go. Of course I made plenty of excuses not to leave at that time. I was involved in ministries that I loved, around people I loved, and I was definitely in a comfort zone. At the same time, I began to realize that the plans God had for me would require me to go beyond the four walls of that church.

The Lord had used my experience in an abusive relationship to set me on the course that He had planned for me. Through study of the scriptures, I gained a whole new appreciation for God's design for marriage. I came to realize how important this singular illustration of Christ's relationship with His bride the Church was, and how important it is for us to carry out God's blueprint for marriage. I had developed a passion to see broken marriages restored if at all possible. I wanted to help those who were not yet married to be prepared by understanding God's design for marriage and the roles and responsibilities of the Christian husband and wife. I wanted to help single people make wise decisions to marry, or as the case may be, *not* to marry, so that they would avoid finding themselves in unproductive, non-God-glorifying, miserable relationships.

I knew that a large part of my ministry would involve counseling others in the areas of relationships, especially marriage. Already, all sorts of people were coming to me for advice: single people, divorced people, even married people. There were many times when I would find myself in discussions relating to relationships. Some of the things I had learned I could freely share, but I could not share everything in that environment. I could not say or do anything that might go against the doctrine of that church or the authority of my Pastor's teaching because that would have only created confusion and dissension. The Lord was shifting me to another level of ministry, and I began to realize that I would not be able to effectively minister to many of the hurting individuals in that church. This really grieved me, but God had spoken to me three years earlier in order to prepare me for the change that He knew would come. I had to finally accept the fact that I had to go in order to grow.

One by one, God saw to it that each of my ministry involvements was transferred into the hands of other capable people. I no longer had that as an excuse, but I *still* lingered on the scene. As time wore on, I finally found enough courage to venture out and visit another church, but I made no definitive move. The longer I stayed at my old church, the more I was beginning to feel as if I was treading in dangerous territory. It reached a point where Sunday after Sunday I would go to church and by the time I left I would be very unsettled. The familiar surroundings that I had grown accustomed to began to feel very uncomfortable.

I remember the last Sunday morning that I went to that church as a member. I woke up that morning with a horrible feeling about going. I just couldn't explain it. I shared with my mother how difficult it was for me to go to that particular church that morning, and she

in transition

suggested that I not go there. In spite of the foreboding feeling I had about going, I got dressed and went anyway. Boy, was that a mistake! It was as if a dark cloud was hanging over my head that day. By the middle of the service I knew in my heart that it would be my last Sunday there as a member. The service couldn't end fast enough for me that day, and as soon as I heard the benediction I practically ran out of there! God had to use persecution to get the early church to carry out the commission given to them in Acts 1:8. I didn't experience persecution, but the way I felt was close enough for me!

I set out, not knowing where I was going, and started visiting churches. Once again the Lord used the example of Abraham to encourage me. I read in Genesis chapter 12 how Abraham also had to get up and leave his familiar surroundings. Abraham had the assurance, as I did, that the Lord would show him where he needed to be. Whenever I visited a church, as I entered the sanctuary and sat down I would quietly pray and ask the Lord if that was the church He wanted me to be a part of. For each church I visited, I knew in my spirit that I had not yet found the place where God wanted me to be. I became very discouraged and many Sundays I would burst into tears as I drove back home. I was frustrated and I couldn't understand why it seemed to be taking so long for me to do what I knew God wanted me to do—find a new church home—but God had a plan. Yet again He was teaching me a lesson, and in the end, I didn't find my new church home; my new church home found me.

Some friends of mine who knew that I was searching for a new church recommended the church that they had once been members of. I immediately rejected the idea because I didn't think that would be the best place for me. One of the primary reasons I did not think

67

I could become a member there was that the Pastor had been mentored by my former Pastor, and I did not want to find myself in the same doctrinal dilemma I had just left.

My friends suggested yet another church that was populated primarily with people my age and was described as being new and exciting, so I gave it a try. I went to visit, but again, much to my own disappointment, I left knowing that was not the place for me.

I was in school at the time finishing up a three-year training program for certification in Biblical counseling, and the next evening as I left the lecture hall to head for class, I saw a couple that I had noticed at the church I had just visited. I'm a fairly shy person, but for some reason I felt the need to go by and say hello, so I did. The man was talking with someone but the lady was available so I went up to her. I said hello, and asked her if she and her husband were members of the church where I had seen them the day before. She told me that they were not members there, but the conversation turned and she asked me what church I belonged to. I told her that I had actually been looking for a new church and she promptly recommended her church. She even offered to come and pick me up if I didn't have a ride. It turned out that the church she was a member of was the first church that my friends had recommended to me (the one that I had immediately rejected).

The lady was so enthusiastic and gracious in her invitation that I was persuaded to take her up on her offer. I went that very week, and as I sat in the pew and looked at the people's faces and listened to the songs and the preaching, I turned to Faith, the Faithful Witness (who accompanied me that night), and I said, "I think this is it!" Everything I had been looking for and all that I sensed I needed in a church was there: friendliness, energy, enthusiasm, exegetical teaching and preaching, vibrant and growing ministries—it was all there. But I still was hesitant to join the church because I feared that I would find myself under the same doctrine taught at my former church. That was when the Lord spoke to me. He told me to go to the next Bible study they were having and join the church.

I knew that the Lord had spoken to me, but I was struggling with the "what ifs." What if I found myself in the same situation I was in before? What if I was not able to minister through counseling as I believed the Lord was calling me to do? But the Lord had spoken, and "what if" or not, I had to do what I believed the Lord was telling me to do.

The following Wednesday, I went as instructed to the church's Bible study. In spite of my reservations, I went with the intention of becoming a member when the invitation to fellowship was made at the end of the service. One of the Associate Ministers at the church was supposed to be teaching that night. But just before the actual Bible study began the Associate Minister said that the Pastor would be teaching that night instead. When the Pastor came in, he announced that he was going to be dealing with the life issue of divorce and remarriage. I was shocked! I had no idea that this would be the focus of the Bible study that night. I could feel my stomach tightening in a nervous knot, but at that moment the Holy Spirit whispered in my spirit that it would be all right.

I sat at the edge of my seat as I listened to the Pastor talk about how he had believed in the doctrine of no remarriage under any circumstance except the death of the spouse. Then he went on to tell the story of how he had been prompted by the Holy Spirit to begin a personal study on the issue of divorce, and that by the end of his study, his position had changed. He told of how he had come before his congregation and told them of what had happened and of his new position on the issue. It was from this perspective that he began his teaching on the subject that night. I listened in amazement as he went through each scripture I had studied. I breathed a tremendous sigh of relief! By the time he was finished teaching, all of my reservations were gone. I could hardly wait until the invitation to fellowship was made. When the invitation was finally made, my hand was probably the first up in the air. I was able to accept membership with a clear and joyful heart. The Holy Spirit had counseled me well: it *was* going to be all right.

No wonder the scripture says that we shouldn't lean on our own understanding or be wise in our own eyes. If it had been left up to me, I would have never even visited that wonderful place that became my new church home. Not only did I find a great place to worship and to grow, but also I soon became a part of a ministry whose primary purpose was to minister to people who were separated, divorced, or widowed. The ministry focus was the teaching and carrying out of God's blueprint for marriage, one of the goals being reconciliation where possible. I was overjoyed! This was an area of ministry that I had longed to see implemented at my former church. Within a few months of participating in this ministry, I was asked to be the resident counselor. It was yet another portion of God's plan for me unfolding. It was like a dream come true! As if that wasn't enough, the church also had a counseling center and I was also asked to become a part of their counseling staff. I was starting to get a glimpse of the verse that says, "Now to Him who is able to do exceeding abundantly beyond all that we ask or think..." (Ephesians 3:20). This was certainly more than I had hoped for. There were no hindrances to my ministry of counseling and I was well on my way on the path that the Lord had called me to.

By the way, I hadn't forgotten about the "Ram." However, when I became a part of my new church I didn't walk around peeking behind every "thicket" to see if he might be there. That was not my focus. Make no mistake about it, I had my eyes open, but from what I could tell, my Ram wasn't in there. One of the things I did do during my waiting period was to try to learn as much about marriage and godly relationships as I could. The ministries I was involved in certainly helped. On a more personal level, I did everything from reading books (starting with the Bible), to attending seminars, to listening to the advice and testimonies of couples whose marriages I respected and admired. I also took the time to think about the kind of person I thought I would like to have as a mate. Here is a list I compiled which I extracted from my journal:

Things I want in a husband:

He must love God more than anything or anyone else.

He must love the word of God and the ways of God.

He must know his gifts and be involved in ministry.

He must be actively seeking and pursuing God's will for his life.

He must have a passion for young people.

He should be accountable to his pastor and/or father.

He should carry himself with dignity but with humility.

He should have a good report at home and in church, from both male and female.

He should be hard working and skilled in some area.

(It would be nice if he were musically inclined.)

He should be a gentleman at all times.

He should treat all women and elders respectfully.

He should honor self-control.

He should not have wandering eyes.

He should appreciate nature and God's beauty in it.

He should be kind, gentle, sensitive, and a man of discretion.

He should be wise.

He should be loving and affectionate.

He should be committed to his God, [and when he is married] to his wife and his marriage.

He should be patient and slow to anger.

He should be adventurous and fun-loving.

He should have a wonderful sense of humor and love to laugh.

He should be pensive and enjoy times of quietness.

This list was not compiled in a hurry. It took time for God to bring me to the point where I realized that character and integrity are two of the most important qualities you can look for in a mate. I did have some preferences as far as looks, and so on, but those were not the most crucial things. The following section was added to my list as a result of coming in contact with different guys over the years and making note of what I liked and didn't like about them:

He should be good-looking, but not "pretty;" well groomed with nice hands and teeth.

He should know how to dress: not trendy, but having his own style.

He should be distinguished but relaxed.

He must be intelligent, but not acting as though he has to prove how intelligent he is.

He should not be skinny, but if he's really big, then he should be husky and not soft and flabby.
He must be friendly and sociable.
He should know how to make conversation without making a fool of himself.
He must be affectionate (but not inappropriately so).
He should be tactful, courteous, sensitive (to people and situations), and discerning.
He must love music, good books, good food, travel, and broadening horizons.
He must be generous, but not foolish.
He should know how to do some things for himself [i.e. chores around the house, cooking, etc.].

Of course, some of the things in the complete list were required and some were desired, but this exercise helped me to weed out those who did not have "Ram" potential. By all means, we should make our requests and supplications known to God, but at the same time, we must be yielded enough to God that we allow our desires to be conformed to His will for us.

Marriage is too important for a person to compromise and settle for just anyone (especially because we're tired of waiting). If we are going to carry out God's design for marriage then we must do it His way with the kind of person that He would approve of. For us as believers, that rules out unbelievers even if they are faithful churchgoers and appear to be "not far from the Kingdom." A person is either a born-again believer or not. That rules out those who "live right" and claim to be moral people without knowing the Savior of righteousness and morality.

Ladies, that rules out that handsome brand-spanking new

convert who has barely had a chance to dry off the water from the baptismal pool. He's not ready to be the spiritual head of a household yet. Leave him alone and allow him to grow and develop without you being a distraction. If he's the one for you, you'll be glad you allowed him the time to develop spiritually.

Men, that rules out the woman who does not yet understand what it means to be a godly woman and wife (and has no desire to do so). That rules out the woman who is beautiful but lacks discretion. Did you know that such a woman is described as a ring in a pig's nose? (See Proverbs 11:22.) So if you're one that's into external appearances, that might be something you want to consider. In a nutshell, that rules out anyone who is either unable or unwilling to commit himself or herself to carrying out the roles of a godly husband and wife in a Christ-centered marriage.

One very important thing that I did when I accepted God's promise of marriage was to yield my choice of a mate to Him. Sure, I had my list and my preferences, but it was God's best for me that I wanted above all. I told God that I chose the first time and I did not choose well, and I asked Him to choose for me this time. Whenever a gentleman would come into the picture, I would do the same thing I did when I was looking for a new church home: *pray*! Didn't God say that He would give us direction in *all* things if we would just allow Him to? Sure He did! Read it for yourself in Proverbs 3:6.

Every man that approached me was put to the prayer test. My prayer was three-fold. First, I asked God to let me know if this was the right person for me or not. Secondly, if it so happened that he was not the right person for me (or me for him), I asked that the relationship be stopped quickly before any serious (especially emotional) involvement took place. Finally, if the relationship did end (because we were not suited for one another), I asked that God would cause it to end in such a way that neither my or his feelings would get hurt. It worked every time! I never went through any long or involved emotional entanglements because as soon as someone showed interest I started praying, and without fail, God would promptly respond.

There were a few rams that showed some interest, but my Ram wasn't among them. The bottom line was that I was still Ram-less. There were times when I would think about the promise God made to me and I would get very discouraged. I just couldn't understand why it was taking so long for me to meet the right kind of person. I went through various seasons. Sometimes I would be humming along feeling just fine—free and independent, enjoying my singleness—then at other times it would hit me like a ton of bricks that I was Ram-less and I would sink into the pit of despondency. In those dark times I would cry out to God and remind Him (as though He had forgotten) of the promise He made to me.

Each time I became despondent, I would repeat the same verse of scripture that so aptly described my condition: "Hope deferred makes the heart sick..." (Proverbs 13:12). At those times, that's how I felt... sick at heart! Usually when I felt that way, I would ask God to encourage me in some way, anything to help me get through that period until I could hum along again, and He always did. There was always something that lifted my spirits. Sometimes it was a general but obvious reminder that God had not forgotten about me and that the vision was indeed true. At other times it would be something very specific and personal to me to let me know that God had heard and answered my prayer. But even when I had been encouraged, strengthened, reminded, and lifted, I still had to wait.

Have you ever been on an airplane that was forced into a holding pattern? I have. I was on a flight returning home from a business trip. It had been a two weeklong trip and I couldn't wait to get home. When the announcement was made that we were making our descent, my ears perked up and I sat up in my seat in anticipation of arrival. "Almost home!" I thought. But not long after that, another announcement was made from the cockpit. The captain announced that we would be in a holding pattern until they received permission to land. There was no ETA given, and to make matters worse, no reason was given for the delay. We only knew one thing: we had to wait.

It was very frustrating to know that I was that close to home, anticipating arrival, only to be told that I had to wait! Every now and again, update announcements were made from the cockpit: "Ladies and gentlemen, we are still waiting for permission to land. We will advise you as soon as we have been notified. In the meantime, please sit back and relax." What could we do? We did not have control of the plane, and all of the complaining in the world was not going to get us to land any quicker. *We had to wait!* It was not until the pilots received permission to land that an explanation for the delay was given: the President was preparing to leave the airport. In order to protect the President's safety, no other aircraft was allowed to enter or leave the airport until Airforce One had cleared the runway. If any pilot had been foolish enough to attempt to land the aircraft without the proper clearance, I'm sure there would have been dire consequences.

Sometimes God places us in holding patterns. He does not give us any ETA, and many times He does not offer any explanation for the delay. We have to wait for "clearance to land." Sometimes we cause the delay because we are not ready to go down the "runway." Sometimes the delay has nothing to do with us. It could be that there is something else going on at our destination that would make it unwise for us to approach at that time. We usually don't know the cause for the delay until after we have received the proper clearance. If we are foolish enough to attempt to reach our destination without receiving the proper clearance from God, there will be dire consequences.

With the physical airplane, after the delay you may arrive at the airport only to find that your luggage has been lost, or your ride got tired of waiting and left the airport. Things can happen that make your long awaited arrival even more frustrating. Likewise, when God's holding pattern is over, things may not look the way you expect them to look when you arrive.

You may expect that your luggage will be clearly tagged and waiting for you at the baggage claim area. You may expect that the person who is there to meet you will be holding up a sign with your name printed on it in big bold letters. In the reality of God's sovereignty, things don't always turn out that way. You may arrive only to find that your belongings are in a completely different location from where you anticipated. You may also find that the person you thought would be there to meet you doesn't look anything at all like you expected. You may not recognize him at first.

Someone else may even have to point him out to you. He may not even be certain of who *you* are at first!

The bottom line is that things may not work out the way *you* think they should work out. Remember, *don't lean to your own understanding*. Don't get frustrated or fixated on the wrong thing. Get *faith-sated*! Activate your faith! As long as you have received the proper clearance—God's guidance and blessing—He will make sure that things work out the way *He* has planned. Rest assured that God knows what He's doing and that you are in His will.

9

amongfriends

Sometimes it seems that others are more anxious for you to meet that special someone than you are. I've lost count of the many times that family or friends tried to "hook me up" with someone. During the time I had resigned myself to remaining single, whenever someone tried to get me to meet a gentleman of their choosing, my response was always the same: "Sorry, I'm not interested. I'm dead to that." My family and many of my friends had heard this response from me before (the persistent ones had heard it several times), but at that time only a few of them understood why I responded the way I did.

When I became a member of my former church, even though I submitted myself to the doctrine concerning divorce and remarriage that was taught there, the stigma that was attached to those who had been divorced could not be ignored. Most of the people I hung out with had never been married before, but there were one or two that had. Many times when a group of us would get together, a conversation about marriage or developing a relationship would start up and a vigorous discussion would ensue. If a previously married person was there and dared to share a desire to be married again, a strange and uncomfortable hush would usually follow. One lady described her experience in such settings as feeling like she had a scarlet letter across her chest: 'D' for 'Divorced'. I was inclined to agree.

It was because of that type of atmosphere that I chose to be discrete about sharing my own experience. I was not in any hurry to make the fact that I had been married public knowledge. Even during the time when I had no intention or thought of remarrying, I could not bear the thought of being treated like a "social leper." It was hard enough for me to deal with what I had gone through without having to deal with that sort of alienation. It wasn't until I had finished my study of marriage, divorce and remarriage that I shared my own marital experience with my closest friends from that church. The truth I had learned had made me free and gave me the courage to share what had been a very painful experience for me. Fortunately for me, I was (and still am) blessed to have the kind of friends who could appreciate how difficult it was for me to share something like that, especially in that environment. Their expressions of love, encouragement, and assurance of continued friendship was a source of great healing for me.

Before that time of sharing, when I was still a member of my former church, some friends of mine invited me to attend the 1994 Northeast Regional Music Workshop. Since I loved to sing, I gladly accepted the invitation. On the first day of the workshop, my friends and I made our way down the hotel corridor to the first rehearsal. As we were walking, one of my friends had what she apparently thought was an important revelation. Without any prior discussion or provocation, she excitedly said, "I know a guy who would be nice for you, Aleathea!" Before I could respond, one of my other friends chimed in and asked which guy she was referring to. The gentleman's first and last names were eagerly blurted out with what I interpreted to be an "I thought you would never ask!" attitude. Still no response from me. Obviously undaunted by my lack of response, the gentleman's professional title was added as if to give weight to the (unsolicited) information already given. Finally I responded. I smiled, and with an air of finality gave my usual response: "Sorry, I'm not interested. I'm dead to that!" That put the subject to rest for the time being, and we moved on to another topic of conversation.

Later on that evening, in spite of my earlier response, one of my friends took great care to point the gentleman out to me. I glanced in his general direction (to appease my friend more than anything else). I didn't really see him properly, but I also didn't see the need to check him out any closer. My friend seemed satisfied that I had at least looked.

Three years later, the same friend, who shall be henceforth referred to as "the Social Butterfly," invited me to attend a national gospel music convention that was being held that particular year in Atlanta. The convention was scheduled to last a full week and was jam-packed with workshops, rehearsals, nightly services, and other activities. My work schedule had been hectic and very tiring leading up to the week of the convention, but I looked forward to going. By the time I arrived, I was tired to the bone and mentally and emotionally *drained!* The fact that one of the choirs I would be rehearsing with held rehearsals close to midnight did not help my situation, but I did my best to press my way each night.

The late night schedule took its toll on my already tired body, and by mid-week I was a mere shadow of my former self. I generally woke up with two main objectives: 1) to eat, and 2) to get back to sleep as soon as possible. It didn't help that the Social Butterfly (who was also one of my room-mates) knew everybody and seemed to want me to know everybody too. I really was not up to meeting so many people as baggy-eyed and weary as I looked and felt. My eyes were so bloodshot, I really couldn't see much anyway!

One afternoon a small group of us broke away from our busy schedule to have lunch together. There were five of us including myself. Three of the other people were friends from my church. There was also a gentleman among us who I did not know (a friend of the Social Butterfly of course). Unfortunately for him, and much to my dismay, he sat directly across from me. Since I had not eaten yet, I was not feeling very sociable. To make matters worse, it felt like there were varicose veins on my eyeballs. I did my best to pretend that the back seat of the booth where we were sitting was a pillow, and my plan was to grab a quick nap before the food arrived. But no such luck! The Social Butterfly was at work making conversation and had the nerve to engage me in it!

There are two times when I am my least self or others conscious and that is when I'm extremely tired or feeling sick. During these times I don't care what I look like, who's around me, or what they're saying. This was one such occasion. I ordered some water with lime, which is my usual restaurant beverage, and the Butterfly's friend commented that he thought he was the only person that ordered that. I responded with a casual, "Oh, really?" What I was really thinking was, "Please don't talk to me anymore. I'm tired, and I can't really see you anyway."

He continued to make general conversation, and I responded

only when absolutely necessary (i.e. when a question was directed at me exclusively). I was glad when the food arrived so I could have a legitimate excuse not to talk anymore. Lunch ended accomplishing my first objective: to eat. I headed back to the hotel room, my mind on bed, pillow and comforter, with hopes of accomplishing my second objective.

I saw the Butterfly's friend a few other times after that, either in rehearsals or when the Social Butterfly would spot him in the hotel lobby. We did not speak directly to each other except for one time a couple days later when he called the room to speak to the Social Butterfly. She was busy so I took the call instead. Remaining faithful to my secondary objective had paid off. I had managed to squeeze some rest into the hectic schedule so I was much more alert when I took the call. I couldn't help but notice for the first time how easy the Butterfly's friend was to talk to. He made me feel like he was an old friend and we had a nice little chat.

You may be wondering at this point if I had the Butterfly's friend under the "Ram-o-scope." The answer is no. However, towards the end of the week it seemed as though the Butterfly's friend was in the spotlight all the time. In one way or another he seemed to stand out in the crowd. As circumstance would have it, he had to leave the convention a day earlier than the rest of us. But before he left he called the room to say his good-byes.

When he called, one of my other roommates answered the phone. He did not stay on the phone more than a minute or two, but not long into the conversation, he asked her for my email address. I gave it to her to give to him, he asked her to tell me good-bye, and then he was gone. When I returned to work that Monday

I received an email note from him and our correspondence began. We developed a "cyber-based" friendship, chatting via email and instant messages. We lived in different states so this turned out to be an easy and inexpensive way for us to start to get to know each other.

A few weeks after the convention, he let me know that he was scheduled to speak at a workshop in my area, and he asked me if I would like to "hang out." The casualness of the invitation was actually appealing to me and I accepted. I met him at the church where the workshop was being held. As I sat in my seat listening to him speak, I couldn't help smiling to myself when I realized that he would lose his train of thought every time he looked in my direction. The truth was that I was as nervous as he was.

After the seminar we went out to lunch and then came back to the church that evening for a concert. After the concert we sat talking. We were both very shy, but it was obvious that we enjoyed each other's company. Towards the end of the evening he did everything he could to keep the conversation going so he wouldn't have to leave. I was enjoying the conversation, but by then I was also nearing my tired (loss of self and others consciousness) zone and my conversation was becoming less spontaneous. Once again, I found myself looking around for something I could make more pillow-like. Common sense eventually kicked in and realizing the lateness of the hour, and the fact that he had at least a two-hour drive ahead of him, we reluctantly said our good-byes.

I had not put my new friend to the prayer test before this time because our focus was on friendship, but after spending the day in each other's company, I quickly activated the prayer test. Our on-line conversations continued and took on a more personal tone. As we shared in our conversations we eventually progressed from a casual friendship to a much more personal one. We learned about each other's likes and dislikes. We were both struck by how much we had in common, life-wise and ministry-wise. We covered a myriad of subjects in our conversations: family, scriptures, interests, music, relationships, personality, background, education... you name it! I knew he was taking our friendship seriously when he asked me for my home, work and pager numbers. Our on-line conversations began to spill over into phone conversations and as the months passed the friendship slowly transitioned from casual acquaintances to close friends.

Every now and again he would say something that would hint of something a little more than "just friends." He had survived the prayer test up to that point, but before things went too far I told him that God was preparing me to be a wife, *not* a girlfriend. I had to let him know that any intentions towards me had better be serious ones or he could keep them to himself or direct them elsewhere. He expressed his appreciation for my candor and we continued in our friendship which continued to grow and deepen.

As time went on, it was obvious that the potential to be more than just friends was there. However, because of my past experience and since he was the first man to survive the prayer test, I was extremely cautious. I did my best to hold my emotions in check. I decided that I would not read any more into our friendship than what was expressly stated. I determined that if he wanted more than a friendship there would be no reading between the lines: he would have to make that message clear.

We went out a few more times and it was becoming clearer that there was an attraction developing that went beyond friendship. The looks got longer, and we both blushed and grinned like two innocent school kids. In our continued conversations he was beginning to speak more and more in (what I interpreted to be) terms of relationship. In these instances, I would ask him to clarify such statements. The statements seemed clear to *me*, but I wanted to be sure I understood exactly how *he* interpreted what he was saying to me.

When I would challenge him as to the meaning and purpose of some of his statements, he would sometimes state an obvious interest, and at other times he would beat around the bush and be indirect. He called it "approach- avoidance." I called it getting on my nerves! I began to lose interest after a few rounds of his approach-avoidance tactics. Because he was not up-front with his intentions, I assumed he really didn't know what he wanted from me—friendship or relationship—and his mixed signals were beginning to confuse me. When he wouldn't stop his approach-avoidance techniques, I put an end to our correspondence. I did not return his email notes, I did not return his phone calls, and I did not get on-line to chat with him. I missed our friendship, especially the daily conversations, but I was not willing to compromise my own integrity by allowing him to think that I was willing to go along with an amorphous relationship.

The conversation ceased on my part, but this man persistent! He continued to call, email, and send instant messages, even though I did not respond. I admired his persistence and respected him for still being so friendly towards me even when he was getting nothing in return. I really wasn't trying to evoke any kind of response from him, but he kept trying to get a response from me. But it was to no avail. The fact that he had passed the prayer test was overshadowed by his ambiguity and no longer held any significance for me. I no longer believed that he had Ram potential. How could he? I reasoned that any man who God sent into my life to fulfill the promise of marriage that he had given me would *never* give me mixed signals. That man would *certainly* know that I was *the one*... wouldn't he? That was my own understanding and I was definitely leaning on it. As far as I was concerned, that Ram had been slaughtered!

10

icanseetheclouds

Several months passed and I still reciprocated no contact with my friend. Then one day I got a very unexpected call at work from him. He was in town and wanted to know if we could get together later that evening. I wasn't sure why he wanted to see me. After all, I had not seen or spoken to him in several months. Curiosity got the best of me and I consented.

When we met later that evening I didn't say much. I was courteous but remained aloof and cautious. I still got the impression from him that he was interested in more than friendship, but since he wasn't saying anything about that, I didn't either. Furthermore, I was already entertaining a possible interest in someone else. At any rate, seeing him again broke my "time of silence" and from that point on we resumed our friendship. It was hard to believe that at that point we had been friends for over two years.

December of 1998 still found me in a "holding pattern" and I had reached a low point in my waiting season. Most of the "rams" I had met could not get past the prayer test. And the only one who had passed the test had been slaughtered before he could even get out of the thicket! As my Pastor would say, my *wait* was becoming a *weight*. I believed God's promise of marriage would be fulfilled, but after more than four years of waiting, I was getting weary.

One morning as I sat contemplating my situation, I remembered a conversation I had with my sister, Marie, a few days earlier. She knew that I had been waiting a long time for God to bring the right person into my life. As we were talking, even though I didn't say it, she knew that I was a little discouraged. She told me that although things did not seem to be working out the way I might have hoped, God had something better in store for me. It was just a matter of time. I was greatly encouraged by her words but I couldn't help but wonder how much longer I would have to wait. With my sister's words still fresh in my mind, I picked up my Bible to see if I might find some further words of encouragement. As I read through a passage of scripture in Isaiah the Lord began to speak to me about my situation. He assured me that my season had indeed come and that the vision that He had given me concerning marriage would soon be realized.

Well, that was all I needed. I had heard from the Lord and boy, was I excited! *My season had come!* I took the message so literally that I expected the promise to come to pass that very day! Of course I didn't expect that I would be *married* that day (I'm not *that* crazy), but I did expect that I would at least *meet* my future mate. I went through the day with an attitude of expectancy, just waiting for the "Ram-beau" to be revealed. I thought, finally I'd at least get to see what this man looked like!

After all the years of instruction, I should have known better than that. The Lord had already taught me that when He says something is going to happen, it does not necessarily mean that it will happen immediately. But I was caught up in the excitement of knowing that the promise would finally begin to unfold. By the end of that day, I had not met my Ram-beau but I was not disheartened. I was certain that if it did not happen that day it would happen the next. But it didn't happen the next day, or the day after that. This went on for about a week or so, and then my excitement began to wane.

I couldn't understand why nothing seemed to be happening since the Lord had told me that my season had come. I asked the Lord about it and He used another passage of scripture to encourage me. It was the story of Elijah when he had received a word from God that it was going to rain. Elijah, in expectancy of the fulfillment of the prophesy, sent his servant to go and watch for the rain cloud. The servant went and looked the first time and saw no cloud. The servant went back to Elijah with his report: no sign of rain. Elijah sent him back to look again. Again the servant went back to Elijah with a disappointing report. In spite of the fact that there was no visible evidence of rain, Elijah still believed God's promise. He knew what God had told him and he believed it. Elijah sent the servant back for a total of seven times. On the seventh time the servant excitedly ran back to Elijah to report that he could see a small cloud in the distance. The cloud was the evidence that rain was coming. Not long after, the rain came and boy, did it rain! The message the Lord gave to me was clear: keep watching the horizon and I would soon see what I had been waiting for. I kept watching, but December came and went and I still hadn't seen any sign of a "cloud."

Sometimes when we're looking for something, the most obvious place is where we look last. Those of you who have ever misplaced your glasses may have had the experience of searching high and low for them only to find that they were perched on top of your head the whole time. It's the funniest thing! Usually it takes someone else to point out to you that the glasses are right there on top of your head. Sometimes you find them only after taking a good look at yourself. I do not wear glasses, but I can certainly relate to that analogy. The thing that I had been "looking" for had been right there all the time. I couldn't see it until others pointed the obvious out to me and I took a good look at myself. Even then, it took a while before I could see it clearly. I wonder how many times we have missed opportunities to be blessed because we fail to see that the thing we have been looking for was right there all the time.

A good friend of mine who owns her own hair salon was my hair stylist. Since we lived close to each other, many times when I went to get my hair done I would stay as her last customer and give her a ride home. During our rides home we would usually chitchat about remnants of conversations that had taken place in the salon. For those of you who may not know, the hair salon is usually a marketplace of conversation and any topic is fair game. On one of my visits to get my hair done, the topic of conversation was relationships. Specifically, we were discussing the qualities that we would like a potential mate to have. I was ready for this discussion. After all, I had made up my "what I want in a husband" (required and desired) list some time ago.

As I was swiveled around in the stylist's chair, I began to name some crucial items that I remembered from my list. As I reviewed and elaborated on each item, it dawned on me that I knew a man who had a lot of the qualities that I was naming. I'm referring to my friend of over two years, the one I had left in the thicket. Even during the time when I had cut him off, he had still shown strength of character and fortitude that was admirable. He even demonstrated some qualities that I didn't even have on my list! I made a mental note of my discovery but I still did not put him back in the potential Ram-beau category. I was still watching the horizon and as far as I could tell, there was still no sign of a cloud yet.

On this particular occasion, I was getting my hair done in preparation for a trip out of state that I was about to take with a couple of my girl-friends. The trip was scheduled for the second weekend in January. One of my friends worked for a sumptuous hotel and we had a girls get-away long weekend planned. We were going to pamper ourselves in the luxurious surroundings of the hotel and, if we felt like it, take in some of the city sights. The hotel happened to be located in the same city as my revived-from-the-thicket friend.

I mentioned to him in passing conversation that some friends and I were coming to his fair city. He asked where we would be staying and insisted that I call him when I got into town. When my girl friends and I arrived and checked in, we had barely put our bags down in the room when the phone rang. It was him. He offered to be our official tour guide and we decided to take him up on his offer.

He availed himself to us for the entire weekend. He even left church early on the Sunday we were leaving so he could come and say good-bye. Faith (my Faithful Witness) was along on the trip. She knew the whole history of how I had met him and the turns our friendship had taken. I was almost sorry she knew because she badgered me for the entire weekend, taking every opportunity to point out our tour guide's mate potential. On the ride back home I

93

did a mental review of our weekend, and I had to admit, he had made quite an impression. I again made a mental note of the things I had observed and heard.

After the trip we continued our conversations. I'm not sure exactly what happened, but towards the end of January our conversations had taken a definite turn. Perhaps we had both caught a glimpse of the possibility of something forming in the distance. He was more aggressive, pointed, and direct in his conversation. This time when I challenged his statements he maintained his posture. I was still not convinced at that point that he was *the one*. He definitely had potential, but I was still being very cautious. Then the turning point in our relationship came.

During one of our what had become daily conversations, he shared with me what I had suspected for quite some time. He *was* interested in more than friendship. He told me that he had been searching for my heart all along but he had not been able to find it because I was so guarded. This was a wake up call for me. I was shocked to hear that I was perceived as being guarded so I denied it. He was obviously confused, I thought. To hear that from him was one thing, but then things got even more interesting. Within the space of two weeks after that conversation with him, my sister, Faith (my Faithful Witness), and another close friend also told me the same thing. You would have thought that it was some kind of conspiracy! Four different people, totally unrelated, in four separate conversations all told me the same thing: "Let your guard down."

All along I thought that I was being diligent and "guarding my heart," but the four-fold confrontation led me to do some serious soul-searching. When I thought about some of the things I had said and done to him in the past, I had to admit that in reality I had an emotional fortress up that was almost impenetrable. When you have been hurt, it is easy to put up walls to safeguard against being hurt again. These walls act as fortresses and our pride and selfishness are the sentries. My walls had been built brick by brick. Each brick represented one of my painful or disappointing experiences. Fear was the mortar that held each brick in place. Even though I had forgiven past offenses, I was practicing the old adage "Once bitten, twice shy." The sad thing is, I was not even aware that I had put up these walls; it had to be pointed out to me.

The ball was now in my court. My friend had made himself vulnerable to me and expressed his heart-felt interest. The question was, what was I going to do about it? How was I going to respond? I knew that in order for us to move forward in a relationship, I would have to let my guard down. This was a very scary thing for me to do but I decided to take a step of faith and volley the ball that he had placed in my court. I made a conscious decision to let my guard down and to give my friend access to my heart. You might think that it would have taken a long process to reach that point, but it really didn't. It was a conscious decision, an act of my will. I didn't know what to expect from him, but I knew that no matter what, God would keep me.

I told my friend that I had thought about what he said to me about being guarded. I also told him that the same message had been echoed three more times since he told me. I confessed to him that I had come to the realization that what he and the others said was true: I was guarded. Even though I was not one hundred percent sure what he was going to do with it, I put my faith into action and I told him that I would give him access to my heart. To my delight, he assured me that he would take the utmost care in handling my heart. From that point on our relationship went to a whole new level.

Yes, there was definitely a cloud on the horizon and it was fast approaching. The scripture in Habakkuk 2:3 was becoming a reality:

> "For the vision is yet for the *appointed time; it hastens* toward the goal, and *it will not fail.* Though it tarries, wait for it; for *it will certainly come, it will not delay.*" (Emphasis added.)

The promise was unfolding with breath-taking speed. How quickly did things unfold? Here's a brief timeline. In December of 1998 I did not know who my promised mate was. All I had was a reconciled friendship, a promise, and a word of assurance that my season had come. By the end of January, our reconciled friendship had reached a turning point. By the end of February our reconciled friendship had transitioned into a committed relationship. A couple of months after that, my friend declared his love for me and expressed his desire to marry me. When he asked me to go with him to his family reunion that September to meet his entire family, I knew beyond any shadow of doubt that he meant business. Our relationship progressed in leaps and bounds! After the family reunion, I knew for certain that he was *the one.* By October we were engaged and four months later, we were married. Now that's what I call "hastening toward the goal!"

Don't you ever believe that God doesn't have a sense of humor. He does! Looking back now, I think of how God must have looked down at me many times and chuckled. Here's one incident that must have given Him a good laugh. From the time I had received the promise of marriage in 1994 I prayed that I could just catch a glimpse of the person who the Lord had in mind for me. I didn't necessarily have to be in a relationship with him until the proper time, but I at least wanted a glimpse! Little did I know that the Lord had given me a glimpse of my future mate around the same time he had given me the promise. When the vision began to unfold in 1999, I realized that I *had* been given a glimpse of my future mate— a glimpse I *reluctantly* took, I might add—five years earlier at the 1994 Northeast Regional Music Workshop my friends had invited me to! That hallway revelation had apparently been true! Another humorous twist came via the Biblical account of Abigail that had haunted me for so long. In that account, the man who came and whisked her away to be his wife was named 'David'. Can you guess what the name of my promised mate was? You guessed it! *David!*

When God makes us a promise and gives us a specific vision, we often try to figure out how things are going to work out. We use our finite understanding to try to reason out what we believe to be the "logical" steps leading to the fulfillment of that vision. But there is a reason why God warns against "leaning to your own understanding." The reason is that our understanding is limited and usually wrong.

When it comes to a promise of marriage, we might be tempted to assume that we will automatically know who "the one" is. We imagine that we might see a bright light shining down from heaven on that special person, or that we will hear the sound of harps playing, or some other phenomenal sign. We might put out all kinds of "fleeces" and check to see if they are "wet" or "dry." We may anticipate signs and wonders and all manner of confirmations to precede and announce the arrival of the *promised one.*" But as you can see from my experience, that is not the case.

The journey to the fulfillment of a vision is a journey of faith. It takes faith to *believe* the vision; it takes faith to *receive* the vision; and it takes faith to *hold onto* the vision. It is not faith in the vision itself; it's faith in the God of the vision. Your confidence must be in the One who made the promise. Otherwise, you may find yourself trusting in something or someone else—even yourself—to fulfill that vision. Trying to figure and map out how things should happen makes you anxious and takes all the fun and excitement out of the waiting. God is a God of surprises. He takes pleasure in carefully selecting, wrapping, and presenting the gift that He wants to give to you. He may let you know that He has a gift in store for you, not so that you'll become anxious, but so that you'll know that He is a God who keeps His promises.

It amuses me now when I look back at how I tried to figure things out along the way. I didn't have a clue! Nothing turned out the way I had expected. My promised mate found me in a completely different location under circumstances much different than I had ever anticipated. When we met he was not holding up a banner with my name on it. Initially he did not recognize me and I certainly did not recognize him. Even when we became friends things did not go smoothly. We even had a break in our relationship. But what a wonderful surprise it was to realize that he was the gift of a mate that God had intended for me. I've heard it said that sometimes a vision dies before it is realized. In my case, that seemed to be true.

Several of my friends have asked me how I knew that David was "the one." There is no simple answer to that question, at least not for me. There were both basic common-sense elements and some supernatural elements that led me to believe that he was the right person for me and me for him. Here are a few components that were critical for me.

Effectual fervent prayer. Prayer was a vital element in both my and his discovery. Before we ever met each other, we both had a sincere desire to have the person that God intended for us to have and we were individually praying to that end. We were both willing to wait (though admittedly not always patiently) for the right person to come along. Not only were we willing to wait for the right person, we were both willing to let go of the wrong person if he or she came along first. There are a lot of people who say that they are committed to waiting for the right person who get involved with the wrong person and then don't want to let the wrong person go. A sincere desire for God's will in your life is key.

God-directed standards. Another crucial ingredient was that we both had standards for the type of person we believed we would be well suited for and who would be well suited for each of us. This served as our protection as well as a helpful guide. There were certain criteria that were absolutely required. Since we were both born-again believers, a lot of the standards had already been laid out for us in the scriptures. The scriptures have a lot to say about the characteristics of a godly wife and a godly husband. When deciding on a mate, these characteristics, or at least the potential and the evidence of the development of them, should be there. Other standards were not developed overnight, but by diligent prayer, careful observation, and a willingness to learn and grow in the direction that God wanted for us.

Preparation and re-alignment of priorities and focus. When I purchased my house in December of 1997, I had no thought of moving. If at that time you had even so much as suggested to me the possibility that I would be moving away from church, home, and family, I would have bound and rebuked you! But God was preparing me for what was coming long before I realized it. When I moved into my house in 1997, for some illogical reason I felt the need to keep every packing box, even though I had no thought of moving again. By August of 1998, the Lord impressed on my heart that I would be leaving. I believed so strongly that the Lord was going to move me, I shared as much with a friend of mine who was visiting me at that time. I did not know where He would be moving me or why, but I knew I would be leaving and so I was able to mentally start making that shift.

There came a time when there was a noted shift in my way of thinking. Long before I purchased my house, I planned to make it my goal to make sure that my home was always "visitor ready." After I moved in, as I would do certain things around the house or anything that was household related, the Lord would impress upon me the importance of such things in my role as a wife. I began to realize the importance of knowing how to manage a household. Something as simple as stocking up on soap or toilet tissue or preparing a meal took on a whole new significance. I found myself beginning to pay particular attention to information that related to being a godly wife. It was as if an internal antenna had been activated, tuning me into anything—Bible study, radio program, sermon, conversation—that had to do with the subject of marriage.

I remember on one particular occasion going to a Bible study and hearing the minister teach about marriage. He was talking about how most women only think about what they can *get* out of marriage, but they rarely think about what they can *give* in marriage. That was a new concept for me. His point stayed with me from that time until now. If a godly wife is ordained to be a suitable helper for her husband, it makes perfect sense to conclude that the wife should be able to contribute to her husband in a helpful way. If a woman has nothing to contribute, how can she be a suitable helper? From that point on, instead of focusing on what kind of man I wanted or what he might be able to give me, I began to focus on what I might be able to contribute to a marriage. I got my finances in order, which included paying off all of my debts and establishing substantial savings. I purchased my own home. I also spent time working on areas of my emotional and spiritual life that needed attention. Marriage is a ministry, and with any ministry that God calls you to, there is always a period of preparation.

God's presence and pleasure. There was a certain "stamp of approval" that God gave to us which seemed to signify His approval of our relationship. I mentioned in an earlier chapter that confirmation does not usually precede faith. First you believe, then you see and not the other way around. Each time we took a step forward in our relationship another door opened. It reminds me of an analogy I heard about God's will. God's will was described as an automatic door, like the kind you see at the entrance and exit to a supermarket. It was said that just as those automatic doors will not open unless you take a step in the direction of the door, in much the same way, God's will cannot be discovered until you take a step in the direction of what you ascertain as God's will. As you take a step in the right direction, the doors will open.

A major door opened for me not long after my relationship with David got serious. Without my saying a word to anyone, and without even really contemplating it myself, someone approached me and said if I ever got married she wanted to buy my house. This lady did not even know of my prospect for marriage. She knew that I was seeing someone, but for her to put her bid in that far in advance was truly amazing! That was one problem solved before it ever became an issue.

Everywhere David and I went we received blessings on our relationship from friends and strangers alike. Most importantly, we received the blessings of our families. When I met his family in September, I met his mother, all eight of his brothers and sisters, and a host of other friends and relatives. His family and friends gave me a big thumbs up. My own family (though much smaller than his) and friends also pronounced blessings on our relationship. My mother and sister, who would normally put any of my "potentials" through the wringer accepted David with open arms. Before even meeting David, my father pronounced multiple blessings on me and on David. Even after we were married, while on his deathbed, my father pronounced blessings on us.

When David and I were engaged, we had approximately four months to plan an entire wedding, honeymoon, order rings, and settle living arrangements. Within four months, I had found the perfect dress for the perfect price (which by the way only took me about an hour to find); the church, reception hall, limo, and photographer were reserved; flower arrangements were completed; the wedding party was outfitted (and the eight members of the bridal party were in eight different cities in six different states); my house was rented (to the same lady who approached me months before); catering was finalized; four hundred invitations were custom designed, printed, mailed and confirmed; the wedding program was finalized and printed; and the honeymoon was reserved and waiting for us. *Whew!* It seemed a formidable task, but things came together in a miraculous way. The Lord blessed us at every turn and it was evident that God was with us.

Who could have known that something as painful as what I had experienced nearly thirteen years prior would become the catapult that thrust me towards the realization of a vision. Satan meant it for evil, but God meant it all for my good. God used all that I went through to mold me, and shape me, and prepare me for the path that He had ordained for me all along. Knowing the decisions that I would make earlier in life, an omniscient God decided to allow me to take certain turns and each turn was simply the rotation of the Potter's wheel as He made me what He wanted me to be.

So much good has come out of those painful experiences, I can actually be thankful for them. God has used them to forge character into me in a way that I don't believe any other experience would have. Now I have a sensitivity to marriage that gives me a burden to see marriages (especially my own) fulfilled the way God intended them to be. I've been blessed with a husband who loves God and who loves me. He is gentle enough to be considerate of my past, and strong enough to lead us into our future. He also shares the burden of wanting to see more exemplary marriages in the church and to help single people who desire to be married make the right choices so that they won't end up "wrecked."

The fulfillment of God's promise of marriage has been so much more than I could have ever anticipated. David and I are in our Canaan land, our land of promise. Make no mistakes about it, just as with the children of Israel, our Canaan land also has some giants in it that we must fight (maybe I'll write another book about that), especially with our commitment to have a God-honoring marriage. But it is definitely a land flowing with milk and honey.

God makes promises to us in order to give us a vision. The promise of marriage has been realized completing this portion of the vision God gave to me, but it doesn't end there. The merging of our two lives—David's and mine—has created a whole new vision which will not be complete until we have realized our full potential and purpose in this marriage and for our lives. Because when it comes right down to it, realizing our full potential and purpose is, after all, the reason God gives us a vision in the first place.

Published by Dathea

For more information contact:

Dathea Publishing
6722 3rd Street, N.W., Suite 103
Washington, D.C. 20012
E-mail: dathea@dathea.com
Website: www.dathea.com

To contact the author, please send e-mail to:
vision@dathea.com
or contact the publisher at the above address.

Printed in the United States by Morris Publishing, Kearney, N.E.